Nova Scotia
Duck Tolling Retriever

◇

By Nona Kilgore Bauer

Head:: Should be in proportion to the body size, is clean-cut and slightly wedge-shaped when viewed from above. The broad skull is only slightly rounded, the occiput not prominent and the cheeks flat. The stop is moderate.

Ears: Triangular, rounded at the tips, medium-sized and carried in a dropped fashion. They are set high and well back on the skull.

Eyes: Set well apart, almond shaped, medium-sized. Color, amber to brown. Expression is friendly, alert and intelligent.

Neck: Slightly arched, strongly muscled and well set-on, of medium length, with no indication of throatiness.

Nose: Tapers from bridge to tip, with nostrils well open. Color should blend with that of the coat or be black.

Muzzle: Tapers in a clean line from stop to nose, with the lower jaw strong but not prominent.

Mouth: Lips fit fairly tightly, forming a gentle curve in profile, with no heaviness in flews. The correct bite is tight scissors, full dentition is required. Softness in mouth is essential.

Forequarters: Shoulders should be muscular, with the blade well laid back. Elbows should be close to the body, turning neither in nor out. The forelegs should appear as parallel columns, straight and strong in bone. The strongly-webbed feet are tight and round, with well-arched toes, thick pads and strong nails.

Physical Characteristics of the
Nova Scotia Duck Tolling Retriever
(from the Canadian Kennel Club breed standard)

Body: Deep-chested with good spring of rib, brisket reaching to the elbow. The back is short and straight, the topline level, the loins strong and muscular. The ribs are well-sprung, neither barrel shaped nor flat. Tuck-up is moderate.

Tail: Following the natural very slight slope of the croup, broad at the base, luxuriant and heavily feathered.

Hindquarters: Muscular, broad, and square in appearance. Rear and front angulation should be in balance. Thighs are very muscular, upper and lower sections being approximately equal in length. Stifles are well bent and hocks well let down, turning neither in nor out. Dewclaws must not be present.

Coat and Color: Water-repellent double coat of medium length and softness with a softer, dense undercoat. The coat may have a slight wave on the back, but is otherwise straight. Featherings are soft at the throat behind the ears and at the back of the thighs, and forelegs are moderately feathered. Color is various shades of red or orange with lighter featherings and underside of tail, and usually at least one of the following white markings—tip of tail, feet (not exceeding beyond the pasterns), chest, and blaze.

Size: Ideal height for males over 18 months is 19–20 inches (48–51 cm); females over 18 months 18-19 inches (45-48 cm). Weight should be in proportion to the height and bone of the dog, guidelines: 45–51 lb (20–23 kg) for adult males; bitches 37–43 lb (17–20 kg).

9   **History of the** Nova Scotia Duck Tolling Retriever

Trace the origins and follow the development of one of Canada's native breeds. Meet important breeders and fanciers, and explore their breeding programs and successes in establishing the Toller's purity, preserving the breed's special abilities and achieving recognition in its homeland and beyond.

18   **Characteristics of the** Nova Scotia Duck Tolling Retriever

A retriever like no other, the Toller lists its unique approach to hunting and distinct red coat among its hallmarks. In addition, this is a personable, friendly, versatile and depend-able companion and family dog. Are you the right owner for a Toller? Also discussed are hereditary concerns in the breed.

23   **Breed Standard for the** Nova Scotia Duck Tolling Retriever

Learn the requirements of a well-bred Nova Scotia Duck Tolling Retriever by studying the description of the breed as set forth in the standard of the Toller's homeland, that of the Canadian Kennel Club. All Tollers must possess key characteristics as outlined.

28   **Your Puppy** Nova Scotia Duck Tolling Retriever

Be advised about choosing a reputable breeder and selecting a healthy, typical puppy. Understand the responsibilities of ownership, including home preparation, acclimatization, the vet and prevention of common puppy problems.

54   **Everyday Care of Your** Nova Scotia Duck Tolling Retriever

Enter into a sensible discussion of dietary and feeding considerations, exercise, grooming, traveling and identification of your dog. This chapter discusses Nova Scotia Duck Tolling Retriever care for all stages of development.

67   **Training Your** Nova Scotia Duck Tolling Retriever

By Charlotte Schwartz
Be informed about the importance of training your Nova Scotia Duck Tolling Retriever from the basics of house-training and understanding the development of a young dog to executing obedience commands (sit, stay, down, etc.).

Contents

KENNEL CLUB BOOKS® NOVA SCOTIA DUCK TOLLING RETRIEVER
ISBN 13: 978-1-62187-165-1

Copyright 2003 • Kennel Club Books®
Published by: CompanionHouse, A Division of Fox Chapel Publishing
903 Square Street, Mount Joy, PA 17552
Printed in the USA | www.facebook.com/companionhousebooks

All rights reserved. No part of this book may be reproduced in any form, by photostat, scanner, microfilm, xerography or any other means, or incorporated into any information retrieval system, electronic or mechanical, without the written permission of the copyright owner.

Photography by Carol Ann Johnson,
with additional photographs by:

Norvia Behling, TJ Calhoun, Doskocil, Isabelle Français, Bill Jonas, Mikki Pet Products and Alice van Kempen.

Illustrations by Patricia Peters.

The publisher would like to thank Henk de Wit, the "Newfanora Clan" and the rest of the owners of the dogs featured in this book.

The Nova Scotia Duck Tolling Retriever at work. More than just a retriever, the NSDTR is a skilled hunting helper who uses the unique practice of "tolling" to lure game within the hunter's range.

NOVA SCOTIA
DUCK TOLLING RETRIEVER

The early morning sky fills with a noisy squadron of hungry ducks, circling slowly, cautiously, in search of morning feeding grounds. On the shore below, a red fox-like animal scurries back and forth between the shrubbery, prancing energetically along the water's edge in full view of the ducks, tail aloft and waving.

Curious, the birds descend, drawn hypnotically to the mysterious activity below. They bank closer for a better look. A dark figure rises from the shrubbery, a shotgun thunders and the cloud of ducks explodes, fleeing from their fallen comrades. When the gunpowder settles, the hunter has provisions for his dinner table, thanks to the antics of his animated hunting partner, the Nova Scotia Duck Tolling Retriever (or "Toller"). In an appropriate finale to his showmanship, the Toller then dives into the water to retrieve the dead or injured birds.

This engaging phenomenon has been performed for centuries by the craftiest of predators, the red fox. Today's Toller aficionados often recount how the early market hunters had observed the hunting patterns of the red fox and his mate. When the fox pair sighted a flock of ducks flying overhead or swimming out in open water, one fox began to prance and scamper along the shore while the other hid itself in nearby grass or bushes. The prancing fox had an uncanny magnetic effect upon the birds, luring them closer to investigate this strange performance. The ducks paddled to shore, where the fox's mate would spring from the bushes and snap up an unsuspecting duck for dinner.

How to explain the mysterious magic of the Toller and why ducks would find them so alluring? *Tolling*, as defined by wordsmiths, means to entice, allure or attract. As the tolling of church bells calls the congregation to assemble, so does the Nova Scotia Duck Toller perform to lure his game. Although scientists understand most wildlife habits and behavior, they remain baffled at the chemistry between waterfowl and the antics of the fox and the duck tolling retriever.

Fortunately for admirers of the Nova Scotia Duck Tolling Retriever, the magic lives on in the many other virtues of this engaging little retriever. This most unique waterfowl specialist is also an excellent family companion who is devoted to family and children. Today's Toller fortunately remains one of the rare breeds unspoiled by popularity or overbreeding.

The earliest historical references to the Toller date back to the 17th century and the writings of French explorer Nicholas Denys (1598–1685), colonizer of both Nova Scotia and New Brunswick. Denys does not presume to opine on the exact origin of the Toller, but merely documents its behavior and the use of tolling retrievers in Acadia (the French colony on the Atlantic coast of North America in what is now eastern Canada). Although the practice of tolling with small, reddish or red and white dogs had been recorded earlier in Japan, Holland, France and Belgium, Denys was the first to observe and document such hunting methods on the North American continent.

As to their arrival in Nova Scotia, most modern theorists believe that when the Acadians resettled in Nova Scotia during the mid-1700s, they brought with them their main food-source providers, the little red dogs described by Denys.

During that period, Nova Scotia's district of Yarmouth County was affectionately termed

DUTCH DESCENDANT?

In many circles, the Toller is believed to be descended from the Kooikerhondje, also known as the Dutch "cage dog" in the Netherlands.

the "black duck capital of the world," its grassy marshes offering ideal feeding grounds for this type of waterfowl. This also was a perfect setting for the hunting antics of the Toller, and yet one more factor in the tolling retriever's development in that country. During that time, the Toller was also known as the Yarmouth Toller as well as the Little River Duck Dog, so named after the town of Little River Harbor in Yarmouth County.

As much speculation exists about the ancestors of the Toller as about the breed's history. One fanciful legend suggests a cross-breeding between a fox and a retriever, a colorful tale that has little basis in fact. The fox, in fact, is a member of the vulpine genera, which is part of the canine family, though a canine crossbreeding would be unlikely.

Breeds thought to be in the Toller's background include the Brittany, Chesapeake Bay Retriever, Golden Retriever and small farm collies. The marked resemblance to the Golden Retriever seems to lend credence to the use of that breed some distant time ago. One unverified account of what is thought to be the first attempt to produce a pure Toller dates back to 1860, when a James Allen crossed a liver-colored Flat-Coated Retriever with a Labrador-type retriever. In the hope of breeding a smaller dog of

reddish color, Allen allegedly mated the female pups from that cross with Cocker Spaniels, then later bred to an Irish Setter to produce the red color and finally bred to a farm collie to produce a bushier tail.

The Brittany, previously known as the Brittany Spaniel, is a hunting spaniel from France and is thought to be in the Nova Scotia Duck Toller's background.

IMPORTANT EARLY TOLLER BREEDERS

In all accounts, both written and oral, the same name emerges when discussing the history and development of the 20th-century Toller: Eddie Kenney (1874–1953), a third-generation native of Nova Scotia. According to Kenney's grandson, Frank Nickerson, Eddie was the third generation of the Kenney family to raise Little River Duck Dogs. Eddie held a deep passion for nature, animals and wildlife, and had a particular affection for the tolling retriever. He kept a modest kennel at his home in Comeau's Hill at Little River Harbor, where he lived with and hunted with his beloved

One theory states that a cross between a Flat-Coated Retriever (shown here) and a Labrador-type dog was part of an attempt to produce a tolling retriever.

Tollers. Eddie frequently bred his bitches and, although no factual breeding records exist, it is believed that Kenney's dogs are behind some of the first Tollers officially recognized by the Canadian Kennel Club (CKC).

Although efforts to develop Little River Duck Dogs continued in some corners of Acadia, the Toller lived and hunted in relative obscurity for decades before being recognized as a separate breed. Through the dedicated efforts of Colonel Cyril Colwell (1898–1965) of Halifax, the Toller was first recognized by the CKC and officially renamed the Nova Scotia Duck Tolling Retriever. Colwell, originally a Great Dane fancier, first became enamored with the

Little River Duck Dog as a young man in 1923. From that day forward, the little red dogs became an integral part of Colwell's life, and he was never without a beloved Toller companion. He bred several litters during his lifetime, caring for his pups as tenderly as he lived with his personal dogs. He bred only what he considered to be the best specimens of tolling retriever and kept detailed records of the bloodlines behind his breedings. It is known that he obtained some of his breeding stock from Eddie Kenney.

In 1945, Colwell drew up a breed standard for his tolling retriever, christened the breed the Nova Scotia Duck Tolling

BIRTHPLACE OF A BREED

At the gateway to Little River Harbor and Comeau's Hill, a large sign welcomes visitors to "The Birthplace of the Little River Duck Dog."

Retriever and submitted the breed for acceptance to the CKC. On March 21, 1945, he was rewarded with a letter from the club secretary, informing him that the breed would be recognized and listed under Group 1, Sporting Dogs.

The Colonel's fascination with the Toller led him on a lifelong quest into the history of the breed, and his records provide important links to the early Toller. One obvious connection was through a personal friend of Colwell's father, a flamboyant sportsman named H.A.P. (Henry Albert Patterson) "Harry" Smith (1864–1923) of Digby, Nova Scotia. An avid fisherman and hunter, Smith was also an accomplished writer who wrote for several popular outdoor magazines. He often penned his experiences hunting with the Little River Duck Dogs, and his colorful accounts helped to stimulate interest in the breed. His vivid descriptions of the little red dog's tolling ability substantiate its remarkable ability to attract geese and ducks onto the shore. According to Colwell's records, Smith had started a kennel for tolling retrievers in St. Mary's Bay

and had obtained all of his breeding stock from Eddie Kenney.

Colwell's research also led him to Senator Paul Hatfield (1873–1935) of Bangor, Maine, a respected politician who spent most of his adult life in elected office. Also a dedicated sportsman, Hatfield sought relief from the stress of politics by hunting with his Little River Duck Dogs. During the 1920s and early 1930s, Hatfield developed a Toller breeding program with the goal of having the dogs recognized as a separate breed by the CKC. Like Colwell, Hatfield also had delved into the Toller's past in an attempt to trace certain breedings and thus establish the purity of generations required for recognition. Colwell's research into Hatfield's efforts also raised the possibility that some of Eddie Kenney's stock may have been descended from one of Senator Hatfield's dogs.

Vincent J. Pottier (1897–1980) of Belleville, Nova Scotia, a successful attorney, respected

The Chesapeake Bay Retriever is also thought to have played a role in the Toller's development.

politician and Justice of the N.S. Supreme Court, was yet another ardent hunter who held a deep affection for the Little River Duck Dog. Together with his good friend, Edward Babine, Pottier set up a breeding kennel, using his beloved personal gun dog, Gunner, as the primary stud dog. Possessed of a deep belief that the Toller was worthy of recognition beyond the shores of N.S., Pottier set about touring the sportsman's world, showing Gunner at sporting exhibits in New England. As a result, Gunner was featured in newspapers and sporting magazines. The publicity established Pottier as the leading authority on the breed at that time, and his opinion was widely sought by writers, sportsmen and breed aficionados.

Pottier's partner, Eddie Babine (1898–1981), also of Belleville, N.S., is considered by many to be an equally important influence on

Toller development in the early 1900s. A Yarmouth contractor who specialized in building roads, Babine was a lifelong hunting enthusiast who was well known among family and friends for his devotion to his Little River Duck Dog hunting companions. He trained his own tolling retrievers from puppyhood and prized his dogs as family companions as well as hunting dogs.

During the 1930s and 1940s, Babine raised Tollers with Pottier and accompanied him to the sportsman shows to promote the breed. Years later, Eddie Babine and Dr. Sandy Campbell collaborated to set up another breeding kennel, but the business never became a reality. However, by then, Eddie's ventures with Pottier had already made a significant impact on the breed.

LATE 20TH-CENTURY TOLLER BREEDERS

Of the many Toller devotees who followed in the footsteps of Kenney and Hatfield, Avery and Erna Nickerson rank among the most important influences of the late 20th century. Avery's love for Tollers began early in life as a natural extension of his passion for waterfowling. When he and his wife Erna set out to breed tolling retrievers, they obtained their foundation stock from Eddie Kenney's native territory of Comeau's Hill and Little River

BREED "RESCUE"

By the late 1950s, the original 15 Tollers registered with the CKC had died, threatening to plunge the breed once again into obscurity. The breed was salvaged in 1958 when Hettie Bidewell of Chin-Peek Kennels in Moose Jaw, Saskatchewan, registered two Toller pups named Flip and Lady that she had obtained from the Armstrong family of Bellneck.

Harbor. With an eye toward registration with the CKC, they named their kennel operation Green Meadows, changing it later to Harborlight Kennel of Yarmouth County.

The Nickersons were intent on keeping their pups' "ducking" instincts strong and intact, and, through conscientious and selective breeding, they developed dogs that were known to be intelligent, good-looking and, most importantly, very intense tollers. One of Avery's bitches went to Eldon Pace to launch Pace's Schubendorf Kennel. During the

FIRST IN BREED

Sproul's Highland Playboy made NSDTR breed history on June 1, 1980, at a show in Battleford, Saskatchewan, when he became the first of his breed to win Best in Show.

1950s, Pace and Nickerson kept detailed records of their combined breeding programs in order to establish their stock as pure-bred and merit recognition by the CKC. When their dogs were granted registration status in 1962, only 14 Tollers remained registered with the CKC.

Making a splash with fanciers, the Nova Scotia Duck Toller is a spectacular sight in action on land and in water.

When Pace retired from breeding Tollers in the late 1970s, he gave his remaining dogs to the Nickersons, which thus combined the Harborlight bloodlines with those of Schubenorf and those of Hettie Bidwell's Chin-Peek line.

The Harborlight reputation for excellence grew along with their dogs' accomplishments, and pups from their limited breeding program were shipped to England and Scandinavia. The Nickersons focused their breeding goals on what they perceived as ideal tolling retrievers, capable of working under harsh and difficult conditions. They concentrated on producing top-notch hunting dogs and attempted to place their puppies primarily in traditional hunting homes, with breeding stock sold mostly to American or European breeders.

While the Nickersons' focused on the hunting and tolling aspect of the NSDTR, the breed in recent years also has begun to flourish in the conformation and obedience rings. In 1980, two Tollers made breed history when they were named Best in Show at two separate all-breed shows in Canada. Those victories sparked the interest of serious fanciers and breeders, and Tollers have since made steady gains in areas of competition such as obedience, flyball and agility. Several have earned Canadian Obedience Trial championships.

THE TOLLER ARRIVES

Tollers were first imported to Sweden in the mid-1980s and the breed has become quite popular there, with dogs imported from Canada and Denmark. The first Toller was introduced into Great Britain in 1988 when Geraldine Flack imported a bitch from Canada, with further imports by fanciers Mike French and John Norris.

More plaudits came in 1988 when the Canada Postal Service celebrated its 100th anniversary and issued a new stamp featuring the NSDTR as one of four native dog breeds. In recognition of his lifelong dedication and many contributions to the breed, Avery Nickerson was invited to speak at the ceremony unveiling the new stamp.

In the early 1990s, a prominent Nova Scotia legislator, Allister Surette, began a campaign to have the NSDTR officially recognized by his government. As a government official with an interest in economic development, Surette believed the promotion of the internationally acclaimed Toller would enhance tourism in his country and he introduced a bill to that end. Surette told the Assembly that "the breed has three hundred years of documented existence in this province..." and it would be "...a unifying source of pride for

The modern Nova Scotia Duck Toller is a naturally beautiful, intelligent dog, prized equally for his abilities as a hunting dog and his dependability and loyalty as a family pet.

all Nova Scotians...and a living symbol of our heritage for generations to come." The breed was designated as Nova Scotia's Provincial Dog, honoring it as "the only true Canadian dog, developed in Canada by a Canadian for Canadian hunting purposes."

AWESOME AUSSIES

The first two Tollers to be imported to Australia (in 1991 by Marilyn Kellie of Kelmark), also became the first Tollers to earn breed championships in that country: Aust. Ch. Missionviews Shilo of Kelmark Imp. Can., and Aust. Ch. Ardunacres Jetlag to Kelmark Imp. Can.

CHARACTERISTICS OF THE
NOVA SCOTIA DUCK TOLLING RETRIEVER

Just what kind of dog would dance and prance at high speed along a shoreline, then dive into icy water to retrieve killed or wounded game? The NSDTR is as unique in his personality and appearance as he is in his behavior.

IS THE TOLLER RIGHT FOR YOU?

Tollers are medium-sized, powerful sporting dogs, keen and intelligent hunters who are willing, indeed thrilled, to work in cold, wet conditions. The breed's coat is red or orange, straight and medium-long, often marked with white on the tips of the tail and feet and a white blaze on the chest and forehead. The Toller's is a true retriever double coat, with a harsh waterproof outer coat over a downy insulating undercoat.

Although they were developed as tolling retrievers, Tollers are quite versatile and do more than run about the shore, luring ducks to their dinner-table fate. They are equally at home on land, scenting game on the ground as well as in the air, and are often used in traditional hunting forays. The pride of the Toller is his magnificent tail with luxurious feathering, carried in a jaunty arc high over the dog's back. Experts agree that it is the movement of the tail that tolls waterfowl to shore.

Most Tollers wear an appealing sad or worried expression that changes to intense concentration at the slightest indication of retrieving. Although they are easy to train, they have a high energy level and live best with active families that can provide the attention and exercise that the breed requires to thrive. Like most bright retrievers, they will get into mischief if they are bored or unattended for long periods of time. They take well to obedience work, and some have enjoyed successful second careers as therapy dogs.

Tollers also are excellent family companions, faithful and devoted to their owners and children. They are outwardly friendly and affectionate with their families, but tend to be somewhat aloof with strangers and thus make rather good watchdogs, barking at the approach of unfamiliar folks. They should never be considered or used as guard dogs, however, as such behavior is totally against their non-aggressive nature.

As youngsters, Tollers are easily distracted and have short attention spans, not an uncommon trait among the lively retriever breeds. They do not require harsh training methods; rather, they must receive gentle but consistent training throughout puppyhood and beyond, since a solid foundation in obedience is essential in building a trainable adult Toller. These are bright students who respond well to new lessons and experiences. Training sessions should be upbeat and positive, but brief to prevent stimulation overload. New owners should be mindful that the Toller is primarily a hunting dog, and while they will enjoy activities such as obedience exercises and agility, they may not achieve the same level of accuracy in these endeavors as some other breeds who are better suited to such work.

Although the Toller's fluffy red and white coat is part of his endearing appearance, it can be both bane and blessing to the Toller owner, who is charged with keeping the coat brushed and free of mats and tangles. A good brushing twice a week is recommended to keep the coat healthy and attractive and to keep shedding under control. Shedding is most troublesome in spring and again in fall, when double-coated breeds shed their downy undercoats to prepare for the changing seasons. The undercoat is an important characteristic in the waterfowl retriever, who must work in icy water and cold weather. The heavy coat can also be a grooming challenge when the Toller encounters seeds, burrs and other debris in the field or just in the backyard.

"Smile!" The Toller's expression may be intense while working, but he's also a happy, loving dog who's ready to play!

HEREDITARY HEALTH CONCERNS

Every breed of dog is plagued by certain hereditary diseases, some of which are common to several types or groups of dog. The Toller, like other retrieving breeds, is subject to hip dysplasia and eye problems. To promote the responsible breeding of healthy dogs and prevent the escalation of those diseases, the Toller clubs in Canada and the United States each has a code of ethics that prohibits members from breeding dogs without first obtaining hip and eye clearances.

HIP DYSPLASIA (HD)

Hip dysplasia means, quite simply, poor or abnormal formation of the hip joint that most commonly occurs in large breeds of dog and is known to be inherited. A severe case can render a hunting dog worthless in the field, and even a mild case can cause painful arthritic changes in the average house dog. Less severe cases may go undetected until changes in the dog's mobility indicate a problem.

"Come on in...the water's fine!" A Toller will much appreciate an owner who gives him opportunities to go for regular swims.

DANCE OF THE DUCK DOG

The Toller's "dance" along the shore is in reality a stick-fetching game that the dog plays with his master to produce the activity that will lure the ducks. The owner/hunter hides in heavy brush and repeatedly tosses a stick or other object toward the water's edge, and the Toller is sent to retrieve it. The dog's flashy style, splashes of white coat and jaunty tail entice the ducks into the hunter's gunshot range.

HD is caused by several recessive genes, which unfortunately means that dogs with cleared (non-dysplastic) hips could carry dysplastic genes that may pass on to their progeny. HD can be diagnosed only through x-ray examination. Only by screening several generations of breeding stock can a breeder be better assured of offspring with healthy hips.

While hip dysplasia is largely an inherited condition, research shows that environmental factors also play a significant part in its development. Overfeeding and feeding a diet high in calories (primarily fat) during a puppy's rapid-growth stages are suspected to be contributing factors in the development of HD. Heavy-bodied and overweight puppies are more at risk than pups with lean conformation.

Just as in Canada and the US, countries worldwide have adopted

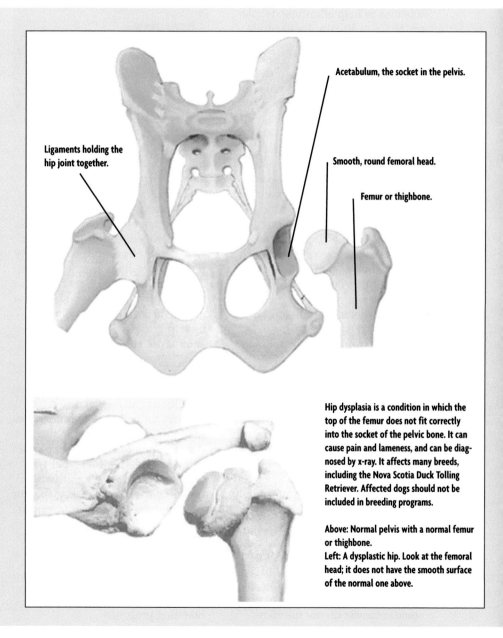

Acetabulum, the socket in the pelvis.

Ligaments holding the hip joint together.

Smooth, round femoral head.

Femur or thighbone.

Hip dysplasia is a condition in which the top of the femur does not fit correctly into the socket of the pelvic bone. It can cause pain and lameness, and can be diagnosed by x-ray. It affects many breeds, including the Nova Scotia Duck Tolling Retriever. Affected dogs should not be included in breeding programs.

Above: Normal pelvis with a normal femur or thighbone.
Left: A dysplastic hip. Look at the femoral head; it does not have the smooth surface of the normal one above.

schemes to help eliminate dysplasia. In Great Britain, for example, the British Veterinary Association has joined with England's Kennel Club (BVA/KC/HD) to help curb the incidence of hip dysplasia in all breeds of dog. Dogs over one year and under six years of age should be x-rayed by a vet. The x-rays are submitted to a special board of vets who specialize in reading orthopedic films. X-rays are assigned a score of 0 (which is the minimum or best possible score) up to 53 (the worst possible score), for each hip, producing a possible total score of 0 to 106. If the dog shows no evidence of abnormality, a certificate of clearance is issued by The Kennel Club. The Orthopedic Foundation for Animals (OFA) runs a scheme in the US in which dogs' hips are x-rayed and graded, and dogs receive ratings that determine whether or not they can be bred.

Tollers who show marked evidence of hip dysplasia should never be bred. Anyone looking for a healthy Toller puppy should make certain the sire and dam of any litter under consideration have the appropriate clearance certificates.

EYE PROBLEMS

Several types of cataracts, progressive retinal atrophy (PRA) and retinal dysplasia (RD) are hereditary eye conditions that can lead to vision problems. While some cataracts do not interfere

DEAFNESS

Late-onset deafness has occurred in a few lines of Tollers. It is not clear as yet whether this condition is inherited or environmental.

with a dog's vision, others can progress into complete or partial blindness. Surgery is now available to correct some types of cataracts.

Cataracts can be diagnosed by a veterinary ophthalmic examination as early as six months of age. Eyes should be examined annually until at least eight years of age, as some cataracts can occur later in the dog's life. All Tollers should be cleared as cataract-free before breeding, and affected animals should not be bred.

PRA and RD are inherited defects of the retina (the light receptor area of the eye). These conditions can be diagnosed only by a vet through ophthalmic examination. Unlike the progressive deterioration of PRA, RD does not result in total blindness, but will affect a working dog's ability to function at a chosen task. Ask your vet about a recent development in testing for PRA, a blood test that can determine with a high rate of accuracy if a dog is affected, a carrier or free of the condition. Dogs afflicted with either condition should be removed from breeding programs.

NOVA SCOTIA
DUCK TOLLING RETRIEVER

Every breed that is recognized by one of the national or international breed registries is guided by a "standard," which is a blueprint of sorts that outlines the characteristics of an ideal specimen of the breed. Standards contain very specific details about the physical properties of the breed as well as its temperament and the abilities necessary for the task for which the dog is bred. These guidelines are used by judges to select the best representatives of the breed and by breeders when planning a breeding program. While breeders recognize that it is impossible to produce a perfect dog of any breed, responsible individuals can do their best to select and breed the best and most typical representatives of their chosen breed, striving to reach the goals set forth in the standard as fully as possible. Without the guidelines provided by a breed standard, specific characteristics inherent to the breed could be altered or completely lost forever.

The standard included herein is that set forth by the Canadian Kennel Club, the national kennel club of the Nova Scotia Duck Toller's country of origin. Although standards around the world describe essentially the same dog, breeders and fanciers are advised to obtain a copy of the standard of their own national kennel club (in the US, the American Kennel Club; in Britain, The Kennel Club, etc.), as wording and detail vary from club to club.

Nova Scotia Duck Tolling Retriever dog of correct coat, balance, type, structure and substance.

THE OFFICIAL CANADIAN KENNEL CLUB BREED STANDARD FOR THE RETRIEVER (NOVA SCOTIA DUCK TOLLING)

Origin and Purpose: The Nova Scotia Duck Tolling Retriever was developed in Nova Scotia in the early 19th century to toll (or lure) and retrieve waterfowl. The tolling dog runs, jumps, and plays along the shoreline in full view of a flock of ducks, occasionally disappearing from sight and then quickly reappearing, aided by the hidden hunter, who throws small sticks or a ball for the dog. The dog's playful actions lure the curious ducks within gunshot range. The dog is then sent to retrieve the downed bird.

General Appearance: The Toller is a medium-sized, powerful, compact, balanced, well-muscled dog; medium to heavy in bone, with a high degree of agility, alertness, and determination. Many Tollers have a slightly sad expression until they go to work, when their aspect changes to intense concentration and excitement. At work, the dog has a speeding, rushing action, with the head carried out almost level with the back and heavily-feathered tail in constant motion.

Temperament: The Toller is highly intelligent, easy to train, and has great endurance. A strong and able swimmer, he is a natural and tenacious retriever on land and from water, setting himself for springy action the moment the slightest indication is given that retrieving is required. His strong retrieving desire and playfulness are qualities essential to his tolling ability. Loving and playful to his family, he can be reserved with strangers without being aggressive or overly shy. Aggression is not to be tolerated.

Size: Ideal height for males over 18 months is 19–20 inches (48–51 cm); females over 18 months 18–19 inches (45–48 cm). One inch (3 cm) over or under ideal height is allowed. Weight should be in proportion to the height and bone of the dog, guidelines: 45–51 lb (20–23 kg) for adult males; bitches 37–43 lb (17–20 kg).

Coat and Color: The Toller was bred to retrieve from icy waters and must have a water-repellent double coat of medium length and softness with a softer, dense undercoat. The coat may have a slight wave on the back, but is otherwise straight. Some winter coats may form a long, loose curl at the throat. Featherings are soft at the throat behind the ears and at the back of the thighs, and forelegs are moderately feathered. While neatening of the ears and feet is permitted, the Toller should always appear natural. Color is various shades of red or orange with lighter featherings and underside of tail, and usually at least one of the following white markings—tip of tail, feet (not exceeding beyond the pasterns), chest, and blaze. A dog of otherwise high quality is not to be penalized for lack of white. The pigment of the nose, lips and eye rims should match, and be flesh colored, blending with coat, or be black.

Head: Skull: the head, which should be in proportion to the body size, is clean-cut and slightly wedge-shaped when viewed from above. The broad skull is only slightly rounded, the occiput not prominent and the cheeks flat. Length from occiput to stop should roughly equal that of stop to tip of nose. The stop is moderate. Muzzle: tapers in a clean line from stop to nose, with the lower jaw strong but not prominent. The underline of the muzzle runs almost in a straight line from the corner of the lip to the corner of the jawbone, with depth at the stop being greater than at the nose. Hair on the muzzle is short and fine. Whiskers are not removed. Nose tapers from bridge to tip, with nostrils well open. Color should blend with that of the coat or be black. Mouth: lips fit fairly tightly, forming a gentle curve in profile, with no heaviness in flews. The correct

bite is tight scissors, full dentition is required. Overshot by more than one-eighth inch, undershot and wry mouth are highly undesirable. Jaws are strong enough to carry a sizable bird, and softness in mouth is essential. Eyes set well apart, almond shaped, medium-sized. Color, amber to brown. Expression is friendly, alert and intelligent. Flesh around the eyes should be the same color as the lips. Ears triangular, rounded at the tips, medium-sized and carried in a dropped fashion. They are set high and well back on the skull, with the base held very slightly erect so that the edge of the ear is carried to the side of the head. They are well feathered at and behind the fold, with short hair at the tips.

Neck: Slightly arched, strongly muscled and well set-on, of medium length, with no indication of throatiness.

Head study showing correct type, proportion and substance.

Forequarters: Shoulders should be muscular, with the blade well laid back and well laid on giving good withers sloping into the short back. The blade and upper arm are roughly equal in length with the upper arm well angled back under the body. Elbows should be close to the body, turning neither in nor out, working cleanly and evenly. The forelegs should appear as parallel columns, straight and strong in bone. The pasterns are strong and slightly sloping. The strongly-webbed feet are tight and round, with well-arched toes, thick pads and strong nails, and are in proportion to the size of the dog. Dewclaws may be removed.

Body: Deep-chested with good spring of rib, brisket reaching to the elbow. The back is short and straight, the topline level, the loins strong and muscular. The ribs are well-sprung, neither barrel shaped nor flat. Tuck-up is moderate.

Hindquarters: Muscular, broad, and square in appearance. Rear and front angulation should be in balance. Thighs are very muscular, upper and lower sections being approximately equal in length. Stifles are well bent and hocks well let down, turning neither in nor out. Dewclaws must not be present.

Tail: Following the natural very slight slope of the croup, broad at the base, luxuriant and heavily feathered, with the last vertebra reaching at least to the hock. The tail may be carried below the level of the back except when the dog is alert when it curves high over, though not touching the back.

FAULTS IN PROFILE

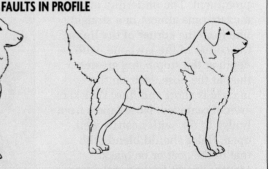

Upright shoulders; toes out in front; sloping topline; weak in rear; cow-hocked; low on leg; lacking substance.

Generally coarse; long-backed; excessive dewlap; short neck; loaded in shoulders; too wide in front; lacking angulation in rear. However, this dog shows correct tail carriage while alert.

Gait: The Toller combines an impression of power with a springy, jaunty gait, showing good reach in front and a strong driving rear. Feet should turn neither in nor out and the legs travel in a straight line. As speed increases, the dog should single-track, topline remaining level, and covering ground with economy of movement.

Faults:
(To be penalized according to degree)

1. Dogs more than 1 inch (3 cm) over or under ideal height.
2. Overshot bite.
3. Tail too short, kinked or curled over touching the back.
4. Lack of substance in adult dog.
5. Dish or down-faced.
6. Abrupt stop.
7. Large, round eyes.
8. Nose, eye rims, and eyes not of prescribed color.
9. Bright pink nose.
10. Splayed or paper feet, down in pasterns.
11. Open coat.
12. Roached, sway back, slack loins.
13. Tail carried below level of back when dog gaiting.
14. Any departure from the foregoing points should be considered a fault and penalized according to the degree of deviation.

Disqualifications:

1. White on shoulders, around ears, on back of neck, across back or flanks.
2. Silvery coat, gray in coat, black areas in coat.
3. Lack of webbing.
4. Undershot bite, wry mouth.
5. In adult classes, any shyness.
6. Butterfly nose.
7. Overshot by more than one-eighth inch.
8. Any color other than red or orange shades.

FAULTS IN PROFILE

Upright shoulders; ewe-necked; weak pasterns; lacking angulation behind; generally lacking bone and substance; tail curled over back.

Long-backed; dip in topline; low tail-set; excessive arch over loin; lacking angulation behind.

NOVA SCOTIA
DUCK TOLLING RETRIEVER

TEMPERAMENT COUNTS

Your selection of a good puppy can be determined by your needs. A show or field potential or a good pet? It is your choice. Every puppy, however, should be of good temperament. Although show-quality puppies are bred and raised with emphasis on physical conformation, responsible breeders strive for equally good temperament. Do not buy from a breeder who concentrates solely on physical beauty at the expense of personality or ability.

FINDING A TOLLER BREEDER AND SELECTING A PUPPY

A reputable breeder is always the most reliable source for a quality Toller pup who is healthy and will possess the qualities typical of the breed. Because the breed is somewhat rare in most countries, finding a good breeder may be a challenge, but a long and happy future with your Toller is worth the extra effort involved in seeking out a responsible puppy source. Vets, breed and kennel clubs, dog shows and outdoor field events are all potential sources of information about Toller breeders.

Most Toller breeders are somewhat particular about their puppy placement, as well they should be. For all of the care and effort that a good breeder puts into breeding and raising his pups, he wants to make sure that they are going to good homes and that they will be well cared for. National breed clubs worldwide operate by strict codes of ethics regarding breeding and puppy sales. As such, breeders are obligated to carefully screen prospective buyers for suitability, agree to help with rehoming if the initial circumstances change and never knowingly sell to laboratories, retailers or people who deal in dogs for profit.

Once you have located a trustworthy breeder, be prepared for a barrage of questions. The breeder should want to know your dog history and what kind of home you will provide for the little one. Breeders typically want to know details...where the dog will live, who will care for it, where and how will the dog exercise, what pets you have owned and own currently, how many children are in the home, why you want a Toller and how much time you have to devote to your new dog as a puppy and an adult. If the breeder shows little interest in you or your family and is willing to sell you a puppy without asking any questions (it *should* be almost an interrogation process), you would be wise to look elsewhere for a pup.

What do you plan to do with your Toller? Even if you have no intention of having a hunting dog, you should still plan on spending time with him in activities that he loves such as retrieving from the water... just for fun!

The breeder should also be candid about health and genetic problems within the breed, especially any in his own lines. No breed is problem-free, and if the breeder makes such a claim, it is best to move on in your puppy search.

ARE YOU PREPARED?

Unfortunately, when a puppy is bought by someone who does not take into consideration the time and attention that dog ownership requires, it is the puppy who suffers when he is either abandoned or placed in a shelter by a frustrated owner. So all of the "homework" you do in preparation for your pup's arrival will benefit you both. The more informed you are, the more you will know what to expect and the better equipped you will be to handle the ups and downs of raising a puppy. Hopefully, everyone in the household is willing to do his part in raising and caring for the pup. The anticipation of owning a dog often brings a lot of promises from excited family members: "I will walk him every day," "I will feed him," "I will house-train him," etc., but these things take time and effort, and promises can easily be forgotten once the novelty of the new pet has worn off.

Toller dog (left) and bitch (right). Much of what your pup will grow up to be is evident in his parents. Be sure to meet at least the dam; if the sire is not on the premises, at least see his picture. Investigate the health backgrounds of both parents before selecting your pup.

Before you visit a litter, you should be clear about the type of pup you want. Do you want a potential show dog, hunting dog or competition dog, or do you want a Toller solely as a pet. Do you have a preference of gender? In the Toller, there are no significant differences between male and female. Differences lie mostly with individual personality rather than gender. The average litter size in the breed is four to six puppies, so there will be some selection once a litter becomes available.

In choosing your puppy, your main concern is the health and stability of the parents and the pups, and you should ask for information on the following issues:

- Do both parents have a hip clearance from the hip registry of their respective country? A vet's statement of good hips is not a valid clearance; the dogs must have undergone the proper x-ray screening for hip disease.
- Have both parents been examined for hereditary eye disease by a qualified vet and do they have documented proof of this?
- Is the breeder knowledgeable about the breed and is he involved in some element of competition or activity with his dogs? Does he belong to a breed club?
- Does the breeder have only one or two breeds of dog? If there are several breeds of dog, the breeder cannot devote the proper amount of time to become sufficiently knowledgeable about each breed.
- Does the breeder have only one (perhaps two) litter at a time? If

YOUR SCHEDULE...

If you lead an erratic, unpredictable life, with daily or weekly changes in your work requirements, consider the problems of owning a puppy. The new puppy has to be fed regularly, socialized (loved, petted, handled, introduced to other people) and, most importantly, allowed to go outdoors for house-training. As the dog gets older, he can be more tolerant of deviations in his feeding and relief schedule.

A HEALTHY PUP
You should not even think about buying a puppy that looks sick, undernourished, overly frightened or nervous. Sometimes a timid puppy will warm up to you after a 30-minute "let's-get-acquainted" session.

there is more than one litter, it is very difficult to give the pups the time and attention that they need.

- How often is the dam bred? If bred every heat cycle, this is too often and may indicate that profit is the primary motive for breeding.
- Does the breeder have a written contract, and does the contract include a breeding restriction with a mandatory spay/neuter provision for pet dogs?
- Does the breeder guarantee the health of his puppy; if so, for how long? Will he take it back at any time for any reason if you cannot keep it? (This is the ultimate hallmark of responsible breeding.) Does the contract offer another puppy or money back in case of health or other problems with the puppy? Many unscrupulous breeders will honor guarantees only after the puppy is destroyed, asserting that they will never have to replace sick puppies.
- Is the breeder willing to provide you with references of other people who have purchased puppies from him?
- Why did the breeder plan this particular breeding between this sire and dam? "He (or she) is a very sweet dog" or similar evasive answers are not sufficient reasons to breed an animal.
- Are the parents of the litter on premises and can you visit with them? The dam should most certainly be available, and, if the sire is not, you should be able to view photos and paperwork on the sire.
- Will the breeder provide you with a three- to five-generation pedigree? Does the pedigree contain any titles before or after the dogs' names (Ch., OTCh., CD, JH, WC, etc.) in the first two generations? The term "championship lines" is meaningless if those titles are three or more generations back in any pedigree. Working trial titles may not always be a reliable indicator of a dog's true worth afield.

Bright, alert and "on the go" describe a healthy, typical Toller puppy.

"YOU BETTER SHOP AROUND!"

Finding a reputable breeder who breeds healthy Tollers is very important, but make sure that the breeder you choose is not only someone whom you respect but also someone with whom you feel comfortable. Your breeder will be a resource long after you buy your puppy, and you must be able to call with reasonable questions without being made to feel like a pest! If you don't connect on a personal level, investigate some other breeders before making a final decision.

Did the dog pass his working tests on the first or second pass, or did it take many retries

before the dog succeeded? A responsible breeder cares about all aspects of the breed—trainability and correct conformation as well as hunting ability. A hunter who is shopping for a proficient Toller hunting partner is well advised to do his homework and research breeders who either hunt over their own dogs or have sold pups into hunting homes where one can check references to verify the pups' performance.

- Have the pups been raised in the home, not isolated in a kennel building or barn, and have they been socialized with children and other people?

- Do the pups seem healthy, with no discharge from their eyes or noses, no loose stools, no foul-smelling ears? Are their coats soft and clean? Do they appear energetic and playful when awake? Are they happy and confident around visitors, not cringing, timid or fearful?

- Have the pups been wormed, had their first shots, had dewclaws removed, been checked by a vet? Does the breeder provide copies of health records and health clearances and literature to help you with feeding, house-training and training?

- Do you feel comfortable with the breeder? Do you feel pressured or intimidated? Can you ask questions without feeling like you are stupid or imposing? Will the breeder be available to answer questions at any time for the life of this dog?

These may sound like a lot of factors to consider, but you must stay the course in search of a responsible, ethical breeder and a healthy, stable Toller pup.

Breeders commonly allow visitors to see their litters by around the fifth or sixth week, and puppies leave for their new homes between the eighth and tenth week. Breeders who permit their puppies to leave early are more interested in your money than in their puppies' well-being. Puppies need to learn the rules of the pack from their dams, and most dams continue teaching the pups manners and dos and don'ts until around the eighth week. Breeders spend significant amounts of time with the Toller toddlers so that the pups are able to interact with the "other species," i.e., humans. Given the long history that dogs and humans have, bonding between the two species is natural but must be nurtured. A well-bred, well-socialized Toller pup wants nothing more than to be near you and please you.

COMMITMENT OF OWNERSHIP
You have chosen the Nova Scotia Duck Tolling Retriever as your ideal breed, which means that you have decided which characteris-

INHERIT THE MIND
In order to know whether or not a puppy will fit into your lifestyle, you need to assess his personality. A good way to do this is to interact with his parents. Your pup inherits not only his appearance but also his personality traits and temperament from the sire and dam.

tics you want in a dog and what type of dog will best fit into your family and lifestyle. If you have selected a breeder, you have gone a step further—you have done your research and found a responsible, conscientious person who breeds quality Tollers and who should be a reliable source of help as you and your puppy adjust to life together. If you have observed a litter in action, you have obtained a firsthand look at the dynamics of a puppy "pack" and, thus, you have learned about each pup's individual personality—

Beauty, ability, personality and friendship are what potential owners have to look forward to in purchasing a Nova Scotia Duck Toller.

perhaps you have even found one that particularly appeals to you.

However, even if you have not yet found the Toller puppy of your dreams, observing pups will help you learn to recognize certain behavior and to determine what a pup's behavior indicates about his temperament. You will be able to pick out which pups are the leaders, which ones are

PUPPY PERSONALITY

When a litter becomes available to you, choosing a pup out of all those adorable faces will not be an easy task! Sound temperament is of utmost importance, but each pup has its own personality and some may be better suited to you than others. A feisty, independent pup will do well in a home with older children and adults, while quiet, shy puppies will thrive in a home with minimal noise and distractions. Your breeder knows the pups best and should be able to guide you in the right direction.

less outgoing, confident, shy, playful, friendly, dominant, etc. Equally as important, you will learn to recognize what a healthy pup should look and act like. All of these things will help you in your search, and when you find the Toller that was meant for you, you will know it!

Researching your breed, selecting a responsible breeder and observing as many pups as possible are all important steps on the way to dog ownership. It may seem like a lot of effort…and you have not even taken the pup home yet! Remember, though, you cannot be too careful when it comes to deciding on the type of dog you want and finding out about your prospective pup's background.

Buying a puppy is not—or *should* not be—just a whimsical purchase. This is one instance in which you actually do get to choose your own family! You may be thinking that buying a puppy should be fun—it should not be so serious and so much work. Keep in mind that your puppy is not a cuddly stuffed toy or decorative lawn ornament; rather, he is a living creature that will become a real member of your family. You will come to realize that, while buying a puppy is a pleasurable and exciting endeavor, it is not something to be taken lightly. Relax…the fun will start when the pup comes home!

Always keep in mind that a puppy is nothing more than a baby in a furry disguise…a baby who is virtually helpless in a human world and who trusts his owner for fulfillment of his basic needs for survival. In addition to food, water and shelter, your pup needs care, protection, guidance and love. If you are not prepared to commit to this, then you are not prepared to own a dog.

"Wait a minute," you say. "How hard could this be? All of my neighbors own dogs and they seem to be doing just fine. Why should I have to worry about all of this?" Well, you should not worry about it; in fact, you will probably find that once your Toller pup gets used to his new home, he will fall into his place in the family quite naturally. However, it never hurts to emphasize the commitment of dog ownership. With some time and patience, it is really not too difficult to raise a curious and exuberant Toller pup to be a well-adjusted and well-mannered adult dog—a dog that could be your most loyal friend.

PREPARING PUPPY'S PLACE IN YOUR HOME

Researching your breed and finding a breeder are only two aspects of the "homework" you will have to do before taking your Toller puppy home. You will also have to prepare your home and family

TIME TO GO HOME
Breeders rarely release puppies until they are eight to ten weeks of age. This is an acceptable age for most breeds of dog, excepting toy breeds, which are not released until around 12 weeks, given their petite sizes. If a breeder has a puppy that is 12 weeks of age or older, it is likely well socialized and house-trained. Be sure that it is otherwise healthy before deciding to take it home.

Prepare your home and yard before your puppy comes home, as one of your young Toller's first priorities will be exploring his new domain.

for the new addition. Much as you would prepare a nursery for a newborn baby, you will need to designate a place in your home that will be the puppy's own. How you prepare your home will depend on how much freedom the dog will be allowed. Whatever you decide, you must ensure that he has a place that he can "call his own."

When you take your new puppy into your home, you are bringing him into what will become his home as well. Obviously, you did not buy a puppy with the intentions of catering to his every whim and allowing him to "rule the roost," but in order for a puppy to grow into a stable, well-adjusted dog, he has to feel comfortable in his surroundings. Remember, he is leaving the warmth and security of his mother and littermates, as well as the familiarity of the only place he has ever known, so it is important to make his transition as easy as possible.

By preparing a place in your home for the puppy, you are

ADJUSTMENT PERIOD

It will take at least two weeks for your puppy to become accustomed to his new surroundings. Give him lots of love, attention, handling, frequent opportunities to relieve himself, a diet he likes to eat and a place he can call his own.

FEEDING TIPS

The cost of food must be mentioned. All dogs need a good-quality food with an adequate supply of protein to develop their bones and muscles properly. Most dogs are not picky eaters but, unless fed properly, can quickly succumb to skin problems.

You will probably start feeding your pup the same food that he has been getting from the breeder; the breeder should give you a few days' supply to start you off. Although you should not give your pup too many treats, you will want to have puppy treats on hand for coaxing, training, rewards, etc. Be careful, though, as a small pup's calorie requirements are relatively low and a few treats can add up to almost a full day's worth of calories.

Your local pet shop should have a wide variety of crates from which you can select the crate best suited to your needs. Select a crate for your Toller pup that is large enough to accommodate him at his adult size.

PHOTO COURTESY OF DOSKOCIL

making him feel as welcome as possible in a strange new place. It should not take him long to get used to it, but the sudden shock of being transplanted is somewhat traumatic for a young pup. Imagine how a small child would feel in the same situation—that is how your puppy must be feeling. It is up to you to reassure him and to let him know, "Little duck dog, you are going to like it here!"

WHAT YOU SHOULD BUY

CRATE

To someone unfamiliar with the use of crates in dog training, it may seem like punishment to shut a dog in a crate, but this is not the case at all. More and more breeders and trainers around the world are recommending crates as preferred tools for pet puppies as well as show puppies.

Crates are not cruel—crates have many humane and highly effective uses in dog care and training. For example, crate training is a popular and very successful house-training method. In addition, a crate can keep your dog safe during travel and, perhaps most importantly, a crate provides your dog with a place of his own in your home. It serves as a "doggie bedroom" of sorts—your Toller can curl up in his crate when he wants to sleep or when he just needs a break. Many dogs sleep in their crates overnight. With soft bedding and his favorite toy, a crate becomes a cozy pseudo-den for your dog. Like his ancestors, he too will seek out the comfort and retreat of a den—you just happen to be providing him with something a little more luxurious than what his early ancestors enjoyed.

As far as purchasing a crate, the type that you buy is up to you. It will most likely be one of the two most popular types: wire or fiberglass. There are advantages and disadvantages to each type. For example, a wire crate is more open, allowing the air to flow through and affording the dog a view of what is going on around him, while a fiberglass crate is sturdier. Both can double as travel crates, providing protection for the dog, although it is typically recommended to use a wire crate in the home and fiberglass crate for travel.

The size of the crate is another thing to consider. Puppies do not stay puppies forever—in fact, sometimes it seems as if they grow right before your eyes. A small crate may be fine for a very young Toller pup, but it will not do him much good for long! Unless you have the money and the inclination to buy a new crate every time your pup has a growth spurt, it is better to get one that will accommodate your dog both as a pup and at full size. A medium- to large-size crate will be necessary for a full-grown Nova Scotia Duck Tolling Retriever, who stands approximately 20 inches high.

BEDDING

A soft crate pad will help the dog feel more at home, and you may also like to give him a small blanket. First, this will take the place of the leaves, twigs, etc., that the pup would use in the wild to make a den; the pup can

CRATE TRAINING TIPS

During crate training, you should partition off the section of the crate in which the pup stays. If he is given too big an area, this will hinder your training efforts. Crate training is based on the fact that a dog does not like to soil his sleeping quarters, so it is ineffective to keep a pup in an area that is so big that he can eliminate in one end and get far enough away from it to sleep. Also, you want to make the crate den-like for the pup. Bedding and a favorite toy will make the crate cozy for the small pup; as he grows, you will adjust the partition to make more room. It will take some coaxing at first, but be patient. Given some time to get used to it, your pup will adapt to his new home-within-a-home quite nicely.

TOYS, TOYS, TOYS!

With a big variety of dog toys available, and so many that look like they would be a lot of fun for a dog, be careful in your selection. It is amazing what a set of puppy teeth can do to an innocent-looking toy; so, obviously, safety is a major consideration. Be sure to choose the most durable products that you can find. Hard nylon bones and toys are a safe bet, and many of them are offered in different scents and flavors that will be sure to capture your dog's attention. It is always fun to play a game of fetch with your dog, and there are balls and flying discs that are specially made to withstand dog teeth.

make his own "burrow" in the crate. Although your pup is far removed from his den-making ancestors, the denning instinct is still a part of his genetic makeup. Second, until you take your pup home, he has been sleeping amid the warmth of his mother and littermates, and while a blanket is not the same as a warm, breathing body, it still provides heat and something with which to snuggle. You will want to wash your pup's bedding frequently in case he has a potty "accident" in his crate, and replace or remove any bedding that becomes ragged and starts to fall apart.

Toys

Toys are a must for dogs of all ages, especially for curious playful pups. Puppies are the "children" of the dog world, and what child does not love toys? Chew toys provide enjoyment for both dog and owner—your dog will enjoy playing with his favorite toys, while you will enjoy the fact that they distract him from chewing on your expensive shoes and leather sofa. Puppies love to chew; in fact, chewing is a physical need for pups as they are teething, and everything looks appetizing! The full range of your possessions—from old dish rag to Oriental carpet—are fair game in the eyes of a teething pup. Puppies are not all that discern-

ing when it comes to finding something literally to "sink their teeth into"—everything tastes great!

Tollers are not notorious chewers, but they are insatiable retrievers and will certainly enjoy toys to play with. Suitable chew toys include sturdy nylon bones and hard sterile bones. Soft stuffed toys are fine for pups (under supervision), but breeders discourage giving stuffed toys to adult Tollers, because they can become de-stuffed in no time. The overly excited dog may ingest the stuffing, which is neither nutritious nor digestible.

Similarly, squeaky toys are quite popular, but should be avoided to stay on the safe side.

Perhaps a squeaky toy can be used as an aid in training, but not for free play. If a pup "disembowels" one of these, the small plastic squeaker inside can be dangerous if swallowed. Monitor the condition of all your Toller's toys carefully and get rid of any that have been chewed to the point of becoming potentially dangerous.

Be careful of natural bones, which have a tendency to splinter into sharp, dangerous pieces. Also be careful of rawhide, which can turn into pieces that are easy to swallow and become a mushy mess on your carpet.

Purchase a sturdy lead for your Toller's routine walks.

TEETHING TIP
Puppies like soft toys for chewing. Because they are teething, soft items like stuffed toys soothe their aching gums, but be sure to monitor your pup when he's playing with a potentially destructible (and thus potentially dangerous) toy.

CHOOSE AN APPROPRIATE COLLAR

The **BUCKLE COLLAR** is the standard collar used for everyday purposes. Be sure that you adjust the buckle on growing puppies. Check it every day. It can become too tight overnight! These collars can be made of leather or nylon. Attach your dog's identification tags to this collar.

The **CHOKE COLLAR** is constructed of highly polished steel so that it slides easily through the stainless steel loop. The idea is that the dog controls the pressure around his neck and he will stop pulling if the collar becomes uncomfortable. It is used *only* for training and should *never* be left on a dog.

The **HALTER** is for a trained dog that has to be restrained to prevent running away, chasing a cat and the like. Considered the most humane of all collars, it is frequently used on smaller dogs on which collars are not comfortable.

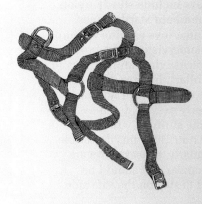

LEAD

A nylon lead is probably the best option, as it is the most resistant to puppy teeth should your pup take a liking to chewing on his lead. Of course, this is a habit that should be nipped in the bud, but, if your pup likes to chew on his lead, he has a very slim chance of being able to chew through the strong nylon. Nylon leads are also lightweight, which is good for a young Toller who is just getting used to the idea of walking on a lead. For everyday walking and safety purposes, the nylon lead is a good choice.

As your pup grows up and gets used to walking on the lead, and can do it politely, you may want to purchase a flexible lead. These leads allow you to extend the length to give the dog a broader area to explore or to shorten the length to keep the dog near you. Of course, there are leads designed for training purposes and specially made harnesses sometimes worn by working dogs, but these are not necessary for routine walks.

COLLAR

Your pup should get used to wearing a collar all the time since you will want to attach his ID tags to it; plus, you have to attach the lead to something! A lightweight nylon collar is a good choice. Make certain that the collar fits snugly enough so that the pup cannot wriggle out of it, but is

Select appropriately sized, durable and easy-to-clean food and water bowls for your Toller. Look into purchasing bowl stands as well, as elevating the bowls is a good preventative against deadly bloat.

PHOTO COURTESY OF MIKKI PET PRODUCTS.

It is your responsibility to clean up after your dog has relieved himself. Pet shops have various aids to assist in the cleanup job.

loose enough so that it will not be uncomfortably tight around the pup's neck. You should be able to fit a finger between the pup's neck and the collar. It may take some time for your pup to get used to wearing the collar, but soon he will not even notice that it is there. Collars for training, such as choke collars, should *only* be used by someone who knows how to use them properly and with correct timing. These collars are for training purposes only.

FOOD AND WATER BOWLS

Your pup will need two bowls, one for food and one for water. You may want two sets of bowls, one for indoors and one for outdoors, depending on where the dog will be fed and where he will be spending time. Stainless steel

or sturdy plastic bowls are popular choices. Plastic bowls are more chewable, but dogs tend not to chew on the steel variety, which can be sterilized. It is important to buy sturdy bowls since anything is in danger of being chewed by puppy teeth and you do not want your dog to be constantly chewing apart his bowl (for his safety and for your wallet!).

CLEANING SUPPLIES

Until a pup is house-trained, you will be doing a lot of cleaning. "Accidents" will occur, which is acceptable in the beginning stages of toilet training because the puppy does not know any better. All you can do is be prepared to clean up any accidents as soon as they happen. Old bath towels, paper towels, newspapers and a safe disinfectant are good to have on hand.

BEYOND THE BASICS

The items previously discussed are the bare necessities. You will

NATURAL TOXINS

Examine your grass and landscaping before bringing your puppy home. Many varieties of plants have leaves, stems or flowers that are toxic if ingested, and you can depend on a curious puppy to investigate them. Ask your vet for information on poisonous plants or research them at your library.

SKULL & CROSSBONES

Thoroughly puppy-proof your house before bringing your puppy home. Never use cockroach or rodent poisons or plant fertilizers in any area accessible to the puppy. Avoid the use of toilet cleaners. Most dogs are born with "toilet-bowl sonar" and will take a drink if the lid is left open. Also keep the trash secured and out of reach.

find out what else you need as you go along—grooming supplies, flea/tick protection, baby gates to partition a room, etc. These things will vary depending on your situation, but it is important that you have everything you need to feed and make your Toller comfortable in his first few days at home.

PUPPY-PROOFING YOUR HOME
Aside from making sure that your Toller will be comfortable in your home, you also have to make sure that your home is safe for your Toller. This means taking precautions that your pup will not get into anything he should not get into and that there is nothing within his reach that may harm him should he sniff it, chew it, inspect it, etc. This probably seems obvious since, while you are primarily concerned with your pup's safety, at the same time you do not want your belongings to be ruined. Breakables should be

placed out of reach if your dog is to have full run of the house. If he is to be limited to certain places within the house, keep any potentially dangerous items in the "off-limits" areas.

An electrical cord can pose a danger should the puppy decide to taste it—and who is going to convince a pup that it would not make a great chew toy? Cords and wires should be fastened tightly against the wall to keep them from puppy teeth. If your dog is going to spend time in a crate, make sure

that there is nothing near his crate that he can reach if he sticks his curious little nose or paws through the openings. Just as you would with a child, keep all household cleaners and chemicals where the pup cannot reach them.

It is also important to make sure that the outside of your home is safe. Of course, your puppy should never be unsupervised, but a pup let loose in the yard will want to run and

Protective wire or fencing will keep your plants safe from puppy teeth and your puppy safe from possibly ingesting something toxic.

CHEMICAL TOXINS
Scour your garage for potential puppy dangers. Remove weed killers, pesticides and antifreeze materials. Antifreeze is highly toxic and just a few drops can kill a puppy or an adult dog. The sweet taste attracts the animal, who will quickly consume it from the floor or pavement.

"Is this for me?" A puppy checks out his new bed and a chew toy. Given some time to explore and get accustomed, your pup should soon feel comfortable in his new home.

explore, and he should be granted that freedom. Do not let a fence give you a false sense of security. Although Tollers are not known to climb or jump, they may dig out of boredom or without sufficient attention. Regardless, Tollers are agile dogs, so it is important to have your yard securely fenced with fencing of sufficient height (about 6 feet), which is well embedded into the ground. Be sure to repair or secure any gaps in the fence. Check the fence periodically to ensure that it is in good shape and make repairs as needed; a

very determined (or bored) Toller may return to the same spot to "work on it" until he is able to get through.

FIRST TRIP TO THE VET
You have selected your puppy, and your home and family are ready. Now all you have to do is collect your Toller from the breeder and the fun begins, right? Well...not so fast. Something else you need to plan is your pup's first trip to the vet. Perhaps the breeder can recommend someone in the area who specializes in retriever breeds or who has experience with the Toller, or maybe you know some other Toller owners who can suggest a good vet. Either way, you should have an appointment arranged for your pup before you pick him up.

The pup's first visit will consist of an overall examination to make sure that the pup does not have any problems that are not apparent to you. The vet will also set up a schedule for the pup's vaccinations; the breeder will inform you of which ones the pup has already received and the vet can continue from there.

INTRODUCTION TO THE FAMILY
Everyone in the house will be excited about the puppy's coming home and will want to pet him and play with him, but it is best to make the introduction low-key

so as not to overwhelm the puppy. He is apprehensive already. It is the first time he has been separated from his mother and the breeder, and the ride to your home is likely to be the first time he has been in a car. The last thing you want to do is smother him, as this will only frighten him further. This is not to say that human contact is not extremely necessary at this stage, because this is the time when a connection between the pup and his human family is formed. Gentle petting and soothing words should help console him, as well as just putting him down and letting him explore on his own (under your watchful eye, of course).

The pup may approach the family members or may busy himself with exploring for a while. Gradually, each person should spend some time with the pup, one at a time, crouching down to get as close to the pup's level as possible, letting him sniff each person's hands and petting him gently. He definitely needs human attention and he needs to be touched—this is how to form an immediate bond. Just remember that the pup is experiencing many things for the first time, at the same time. There are new people, new noises, new smells and new things to investigate, so be gentle, be affectionate and be as comforting as you can be.

HOW VACCINES WORK

If you've just bought a puppy, you surely know the importance of having your pup vaccinated, but do you understand how vaccines work? Vaccines contain the same bacteria or viruses that cause the disease you want to prevent, but they have been chemically modified so that they don't cause any harm. Instead, the vaccine causes your dog to produce antibodies that fight the harmful bacteria. Thus, if your dog is exposed to the disease in the future, the antibodies will destroy the viruses or bacteria.

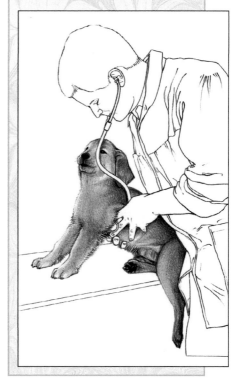

A Toller generally gets on well with other dogs and enjoys the company of a canine playmate, as illustrated by this energetic pair.

PUP'S FIRST NIGHT HOME

You have traveled home with your new charge safely in his crate. He's been to the vet for a thorough check-up; he's been weighed, his papers have been examined and perhaps he's even been vaccinated and wormed as well. He's met (and licked!) the whole family, including the excited children and the less-than-happy cat. He's explored his area, his new bed, the yard and anywhere else he's been permitted. He's eaten his first meal at home and relieved himself in the proper place. He's heard lots of new sounds, smelled new friends and seen more of the outside world than ever before...and that was just the first day! He's worn out and is ready for bed...or so you think!

It's puppy's first night home and you are ready to say "Good night." Keep in mind that this is his first night ever to be sleeping alone. His dam and littermates are no longer at paw's length and he's a bit scared, cold and lonely. Be reassuring to your new family member, but this is not the time to spoil him and give in to his inevitable whining.

Puppies whine. They whine to let others know where they are and hopefully to get company out of it. At bedtime, place your pup in his new bed or crate in his designated area and close the crate door. Mercifully, he may fall asleep without a peep. When the inevitable occurs, however, ignore the whining—he is fine. Be strong and keep his interest in mind. Do not allow yourself to feel guilty and visit the pup. He will fall asleep eventually.

Many breeders recommend placing a piece of bedding from the pup's former home in his new bed so that he recognizes and is comforted by the scent of his littermates. Others still advise placing a hot water bottle in the bed for warmth. The latter may be

PROPER SOCIALIZATION

The socialization period for puppies is from age 8 to 16 weeks. This is the time when puppies need to leave their birth family and take up residence with their new owners, where they will meet many new people, other pets, etc. Failure to be adequately socialized can cause the dog to grow up fearing others and being shy and unfriendly due to a lack of self-confidence.

a good idea provided the pup doesn't attempt to suckle—he'll get good and wet, and may not fall asleep so fast.

Puppy's first night can be somewhat stressful for both the pup and his new family. Remember that you are setting the tone of nighttime at your house. Unless you want to play with your pup every night at 10 p.m., midnight and 2 a.m., don't initiate the habit. Your family will thank you, and eventually so will your pup!

PREVENTING PUPPY PROBLEMS

SOCIALIZATION
Now that you have done all of the preparatory work and have helped your pup get accustomed to his new home and family, it is about time for you to have some fun! Socializing your Toller pup gives you the opportunity to show off your new friend, and likely you will be the only one in the neighborhood with such a unique breed. Likewise, your pup gets to reap the benefits of being an adorable furry creature that people will want to pet and, in general, think is absolutely precious!

Besides getting to know his new family, your puppy should be exposed to other people, animals and situations. This will help him become well adjusted as he grows up and less prone to being timid or fearful of the new things he

will encounter. Of course, he must not come into close contact with dogs you don't know well until his course of injections is fully complete.

MANNERS MATTER
During the socialization process, a puppy should meet people, experience different environments and definitely be exposed to other canines. Through playing and interacting with other dogs, your puppy will learn lessons, ranging from controlling the pressure of his jaws by biting his littermates to the inner-workings of the canine pack that he will apply to his human relationships for the rest of his life. That is why removing a puppy from its litter too early (before eight weeks) can be detrimental to the pup's development.

STRESS-FREE

Some experts in canine health advise that stress during a dog's early years of development can compromise and weaken his immune system, and may trigger the potential for a shortened life. They emphasize the need for a dog to have happy and stress-free growing-up years.

ful during the eight-to-ten-week-old period, also known as the fear period. The interaction he receives during this time should be gentle and reassuring. Lack of socialization, and/or negative experiences during the socialization period, can manifest itself in fear and aggression as the dog grows up. Your puppy needs lots of positive interaction, which of course includes human contact, affection, handling and exposure to other animals.

Once your pup has received his necessary vaccinations, feel free to take him out and about (on his lead, of course). Walk him around the neighborhood, take him on your daily errands, let people pet him, let him meet other dogs and pets, etc. Puppies do not have to try to make friends; there will be no shortage of people who will want to introduce themselves. Just make sure that you carefully supervise each meeting. If the neighborhood children want to say hello, for example, that is great—children and pups most often make great companions. However, sometimes an excited child can unintentionally handle a pup too roughly, or an overzealous pup can playfully nip a little too hard. You want to make socialization experiences positive ones. What a pup learns during this very formative stage will affect his attitude toward future encounters. You want your

Your pup's socialization began with the breeder, but now it is your responsibility to continue it. The socialization he receives until the age of 12 weeks is the most critical, as this is the time when he forms his impressions of the outside world. Be especially care-

dog to be comfortable around everyone. A pup that has a bad experience with a child may grow up to be a dog that is shy around or aggressive toward children.

CONSISTENCY IN TRAINING

Dogs, being pack animals, naturally need a leader, or else they try to establish dominance in their packs. When you welcome a dog into your family, the choice of who becomes the leader and who becomes the "pack" is entirely up to you! Your pup's intuitive quest for dominance, coupled with the fact that it is nearly impossible to look at an adorable Toller pup with his "puppy-dog" eyes and not cave in, give the pup almost an unfair advantage in getting the upper hand (or paw)!

A pup will definitely test the waters to see what he can and cannot do. Do not give in to those pleading eyes—stand your ground when it comes to disciplining the pup and make sure that all family members do the same. It will only confuse the pup if Mother tells him to get off the couch when he is used to sitting up there with Father to watch the nightly news. Avoid discrepancies by having all members of the household decide on the rules before the pup even comes home…and be consistent in enforcing them! Early training shapes the dog's personality, so you cannot be unclear in what you expect.

COMMON PUPPY PROBLEMS

The best way to prevent puppy problems is to be proactive in stopping an undesirable behavior as soon as it starts. The old saying "You can't teach an old dog new tricks" does not necessarily hold true, but it *is* true that it is much

---

CHEWING TIPS

Chewing goes hand in hand with nipping in the sense that a teething puppy is always looking for a way to soothe his aching gums. In this case, instead of chewing on you, he may have taken a liking to your favorite shoe or something else that he should not be chewing. Again, realize that this is a normal canine behavior that does not need to be discouraged, only redirected. Your pup just needs to be taught what is acceptable to chew on and what is off-limits. Consistently tell him "No!" when you catch him chewing on something forbidden and give him a chew toy.

Conversely, praise him when you catch him chewing on something appropriate. In this way, you are discouraging the inappropriate behavior and reinforcing the desired behavior. The puppy's chewing should stop after his adult teeth have come in, but an adult dog continues to chew for various reasons—perhaps because he is bored, needs to relieve tension or just likes to chew. That is why it is important to redirect his chewing when he is still young.

PLAY'S THE THING

Teaching the puppy to play with his toys in running and fetching games is an ideal way to help the puppy develop muscle, learn motor skills and bond with you, his owner and master. He also needs to learn how to inhibit his bite reflex and never to use his teeth on people, forbidden objects and other animals in play. Whenever you play with your puppy, you make the rules. This becomes an important message to your puppy in teaching him that you are the pack leader and control everything he does in life. Once your dog accepts you as his leader, your relationship with him will be cemented for life.

easier to discourage bad behavior in a young developing pup than to wait until the pup's bad behavior becomes the adult dog's bad habit. There are some problems that are especially prevalent in puppies as they develop.

NIPPING

As puppies start to teethe, they feel the need to sink their teeth into anything available…unfortunately, that usually includes your fingers, arms, hair and toes. You may find this behavior cute for the first five seconds…until you feel just how sharp those puppy teeth are. Nipping is something you want to discourage immediately and consistently with a firm "No!" (or whatever number of firm "Nos" it takes for him to understand that you mean business). Then, replace your finger with an appropriate chew toy. While this behavior is merely annoying when the dog is young, it can become dangerous as your Toller's adult teeth grow in and his jaws develop, and he continues to think it is okay to gnaw on human appendages. Your Toller does not mean any harm with a friendly nip, but he also does not know his own strength.

CRYING/WHINING

Your pup will often cry, whine, whimper, howl or make some type of commotion when he is left alone. This is basically his way of calling out for attention to make sure that you know he is there and that you have not forgotten about him. Your puppy feels insecure when he is left alone, when you are out of the house and he is in his crate or when you are in another part of the house and he cannot see you. The noise he is making is an expression of the anxiety he feels at being alone, so he needs to be taught that being alone is okay. You are not actually training the dog to stop making noise; rather, you are training him to feel comfortable when he is alone and thus removing the need for him to make the noise.

This is where the crate with cozy bedding and a toy comes in handy. You want to know that your pup is safe when you are not there to supervise, and you know that he will be safe in his crate rather than roaming freely about the house. In order for the pup to stay in his crate without making a fuss, he first needs to be comfortable in his crate. On that note, it is extremely important that the crate is never used as a form of punishment; this will cause the pup to view the crate as a negative place, rather than as a place of his own for safety and retreat.

Accustom the pup to the crate in short, gradually increasing time intervals in which you put him in the crate, maybe with a treat, and

TRAINING TIP
Training your puppy takes much patience and can be frustrating at times, but you should see results from your efforts. If you have a puppy that seems untrainable, take him to a trainer or behaviorist. The dog may have a personality problem that requires the help of a professional, or perhaps you need help in learning how to train your dog properly.

stay in the room with him. If he cries or makes a fuss, do not go to him, but stay in his sight. Gradually he will realize that staying in his crate is okay without your help, and it will not be so traumatic for him when you are not around. You may want to leave the radio on softly when you leave the house; the sound of human voices may be comforting to him.

A wire crate is good for use outdoors should the need arise, as Tollers like to see what's going on around them. Keep the dog cool, out of direct sunlight, and give him a bowl of water or frequent water breaks.

NOVA SCOTIA DUCK TOLLING RETRIEVER

DIETARY AND FEEDING CONSIDERATIONS

Today the choices of food for your Nova Scotia Duck Tolling Retriever are many and varied.

STORING DOG FOOD

You must store your dry dog food carefully. Open packages of dog food quickly lose their vitamin value, usually within 90 days of being opened. Mold spores and vermin could also contaminate the food.

There are simply dozens of brands of food in all sorts of flavors and textures, ranging from puppy diets to those for older dogs. There are even hypoallergenic and low-calorie diets available. Because your Toller's food has a bearing on coat, health and temperament, it is essential that the most suitable diet is selected for a Toller of his age. It is fair to say, however, that even experienced owners can be perplexed by the enormous range of foods available. Only understanding what is best for your dog will help you reach an informed decision.

Dog foods are produced in three basic types: dry, semi-moist and canned. Dry foods are useful for the cost-conscious, for overall they tend to be less expensive than semi-moist or canned foods. Dry foods also contain the least fat and the most preservatives. In general, canned foods are made up of 60–70% water, while semi-moist ones often contain so much sugar that they are perhaps the least preferred by owners, even though their dogs seem to like them.

When selecting your dog's diet, three stages of development must be considered: the puppy stage, the adult stage and the senior stage.

PUPPY STAGE

Puppies instinctively want to suck milk from their mother's teats; a normal puppy will exhibit this behavior within just a few moments following birth. If puppies do not attempt to suckle within the first half-hour or so, the breeder should encourage them to do so by placing them on the nipples, having selected ones with plenty of milk. This early milk supply is important in providing the essential colostrum, which protects the puppies during the first eight to ten weeks of their lives. Although a mother's milk is much better than any commercially prepared milk formula,

despite there being some excellent ones available, if the puppies do not feed, the breeder will have to feed them by hand. For those with less experience, advice from a vet is important so that not only the right quantity of milk formula is fed but also that of correct quality, fed at suitably frequent intervals, usually every two hours during the first few days of life.

Puppies should be allowed to nurse from their mother for about

The breeder introduces his pups to solid puppy food, and you should continue with this diet after you bring your pup home. Take the breeder's advice on when and how to make changes to the diet.

FOOD PREFERENCE

Selecting the best dry dog food is difficult. There is no majority consensus among veterinary scientists as to the value of nutrient analysis (protein, fat, fiber, moisture, ash, cholesterol, minerals, etc.). All agree that feeding trials are what matter most, but you also have to consider the individual dog. The dog's weight, age and activity level, and what pleases his taste, all must be considered. It is probably best to take the advice of your vet. Every individual dog's dietary requirements vary, and each dog can have different dietary needs at different stages of life.

If your dog is fed a good dry food, he does not require supplements of meat or vegetables. Dogs do appreciate a little variety in their diets, so you may choose to stay with the same brand but vary the flavor. Alternatively, you may wish to add a little flavored stock to give a difference to the taste.

A balanced diet with all of the necessary nutrients is very important in ensuring that a growing pup develops properly.

the first six weeks, although, starting around the third or fourth week, the breeder will begin to introduce small portions of suitable solid food. Most breeders like to introduce alternate milk and meat meals initially, building up to weaning time.

By the time the puppies are seven or a maximum of eight weeks old, they should be fully weaned and fed solely on a proprietary puppy food. Selection of the most suitable, good-quality diet at this time is essential, for a puppy's fastest growth rate is during the first year of life. Vets are usually able to offer advice in this regard, and your breeder will be a helpful source of information as he can advise you about the foods with which he has had success in his own dogs. The frequency of meals will be reduced over time, but the Toller should be kept on a puppy food until around one year of age.

Puppy and junior diets should be well balanced for the needs of your dog so that, except in certain circumstances, additional vitamins, minerals and proteins will not be required.

ADULT DIETS

A dog is considered an adult when it has stopped growing. The Toller usually reaches adulthood around 18 months to 2 years of age, but can be switched to an adult dog food around one year of age. Again you should rely upon your vet or breeder to recommend an acceptable maintenance diet. Major dog-food manufacturers specialize in this type of food, and it is merely necessary for you to select the one best suited to your dog's needs. Active dogs have different requirements from sedate dogs.

SENIOR DIETS

As dogs get older, their metabolism changes. The older dog usually exercises less, moves more slowly and sleeps more. This change in lifestyle and phys-

TEST FOR PROPER DIET

A good test for proper diet is the color, odor and firmness of your dog's stool. A healthy dog usually produces three semi-hard stools per day. The stools should have no unpleasant odor. They should be the same color from excretion to excretion.

DO DOGS HAVE TASTE BUDS?

Watching a dog "wolf" or gobble his food, seemingly without chewing, leads an owner to wonder whether his dog can taste anything. Yes, dogs have taste buds, with sensory perception of sweet, salty and sour. Puppies are born with fully mature taste buds.

iological performance requires a change in diet. Since these changes take place slowly, they might not be recognizable. What is easily recognizable is weight gain. By continuing to feed your dog an adult-maintenance diet when he is slowing down metabolically, your dog will gain weight. Obesity in an older dog compounds the health problems that already accompany old age.

As your dog gets older, few of his organs function up to par. The kidneys slow down and the intestines become less efficient. These age-related factors are best handled with a change in diet and a change in feeding schedule to give smaller portions that are more easily digested. Most vets agree that Tollers reach senior status around seven years of age, so this will likely be the proper time to switch to senior food.

There is no single best diet for every older dog. While many dogs do well on light or senior diets, other dogs do better on puppy diets or special premium diets

such as lamb and rice. Be sensitive to your senior Toller's diet, as this will help control other problems that may arise with your old friend.

WATER

Just as your dog needs proper nutrition from his food, water is an essential "nutrient" as well. Water keeps the dog's body properly hydrated and promotes normal function of the body's systems. During house-training, it is necessary to keep an eye on

Feeding time can reinforce training lessons, too, as this Toller waits politely for his owner to tell him when it's time to eat.

DRINK, DRANK, DRUNK—MAKE IT A DOUBLE

In both humans and dogs, as well as other living organisms, water forms the major part of nearly every body tissue. Naturally, we take water for granted, but without it, life as we know it would cease.

For dogs, water is needed to keep their bodies functioning biochemically. Additionally, water is needed to replace the water lost while panting. Unlike humans, who are able to sweat to dissipate heat, dogs must pant to cool down, thereby losing the vital water that their bodies need to regulate their body temperatures. Humans lose electrolyte-containing products and other body-fluid components through sweating; dogs do not lose anything except water.

Water is essential always, but especially so when the weather is hot or humid or when your dog is exercising or working vigorously.

how much water your Toller is drinking, but, once he is reliably trained, he should have access to clean fresh water at all times. Make certain that the dog's water bowl is clean, and change the water often.

EXERCISE

All dogs require some form of exercise, regardless of breed. A sedentary lifestyle is as harmful to a dog as it is to a person. The Toller is a very active breed that needs a lot of exercise, but you don't have to be an Olympic athlete to provide your dog with a sufficient amount of activity! Exercising your Toller can be enjoyable and healthy for both of you. Brisk walks, once the puppy reaches three or four months of age, will stimulate heart rates and build muscle for both dog and owner. As the dog reaches adulthood, the speed and distance of the walks can be increased as long as they are both kept reasonable and comfortable for both of you. For those who are more ambitious, you will find that your Toller will enjoy accompanying you on hikes and of course will love to take a swim!

Play sessions in the yard and letting the dog run free in the yard under your supervision also are sufficient forms of exercise for the Toller. Fetching and retrieving games are at the top of any Toller's list of favorite things to

EXERCISE ALERT!
You should be careful where you exercise your dog. Many areas have been sprayed with chemicals that are highly toxic to both dogs and humans. Never allow your dog to eat grass or drink from puddles on either public or private grounds, as the run-off water may contain chemicals from sprays and herbicides.

do; these are excellent for giving your dog active play that he will enjoy. Games like tug-of-war, in which the dog can challenge your authority, are not recommended. For games and free running, you must have a securely fenced-in yard for security. You want your Toller to run, but not run away!

Bear in mind that an overweight dog should never be suddenly over-exercised; instead he should be encouraged to

increase exercise slowly. Not only is exercise essential to keep the dog's body fit, it is essential to his mental well-being. A bored dog will find something to do, which often manifests itself in some type of destructive behavior. For this reason the dog's exercise is just as essential for the owner's mental well-being!

GROOMING

BRUSHING
As with any double-coated retriever breed, your Toller requires regular brushing to keep his dense coat smooth, shiny and mat-free. Brushing twice a week is best; however, during shedding season, more frequent brushing is helpful in keeping the clouds of

Of course, your Toller's favorite kind of exercise will involve what he does best... getting wet! If you take your Toller for swims, make sure that it' in a safe area with clean water.

Strenuous or excessive exercise is not recommended for young pups, as it puts undue stress on their growing frames. Puppies do a good job of exercising themselves just by being puppies!

Your local pet shop should have the tools necessary to properly groom your Toller.

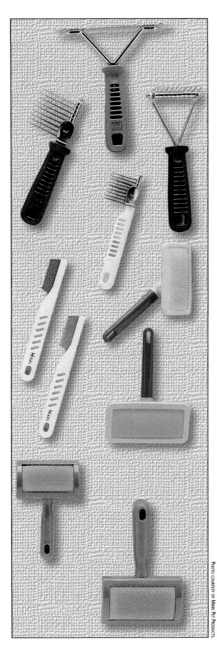

Trimming the hair between the footpads keeps the hair from matting and collecting debris outdoors, thus preventing discomfort to the dog.

dog hair around the home to a minimum.

Slicker brushes work well to refine the coat. If the coat becomes snarled from cockleburrs or other field debris, you might find that using a mat rake is helpful if the slicker brush is ineffective. After any water work, be sure to dry the coat thoroughly to prevent hot spots from developing in moist areas that could fester under the wet fur. The Toller's coat requires little in the way of trimming, although some slight thinning of the heavily feathered areas behind the ears and on the backs of the thighs will help reduce matting in those areas.

Start brushing your Toller at an early age, even if only for a few minutes at a time. Your puppy will come to love the attention and will oblige you by sitting nicely during future grooming sessions. Thus, the time spent grooming your Toller provides you with a valuable opportunity for the two of you to spend time

PHOTO COURTESY OF MIKKI PET PRODUCTS.

together. Many dogs grow to like the feel of being brushed and will enjoy the grooming routine.

BATHING

Frequently bathing your Toller is neither necessary nor recommended. However, should the occasional need arise, it's helpful to be acquainted with the procedure. You want your dog to be at ease in the bath or else it could end up a wet, soapy, messy ordeal for both of you!

Brush your Toller thoroughly before wetting his coat. This will get rid of most mats and tangles, which are harder to remove when the coat is wet. Make certain that your dog has a good non-slip surface on which to stand. Begin by wetting the dog's coat, checking the water temperature to make sure that it is neither too hot nor too cold. A shower or hose attachment is necessary for thoroughly wetting and rinsing the coat.

Next, apply shampoo to the dog's coat and work it into a good lather. Wash the head last, as you do not want shampoo to drip into the dog's eyes while you are washing the rest of his body. You should use only a shampoo that is made for dogs. Do not use a product made for human hair. Work the shampoo all the way down to the skin. You can use this opportunity to check the skin for any bumps, bites or other abnormalities. Do not neglect any area of the

A two-sided brush is useful for grooming the Toller: the bristle brush side can be used for the body coat, while the pin brush side can be used gently to detangle the feathering.

A metal comb can be used on the tail feathering to keep this hallmark of the breed in magnificent condition.

Below: Brush your dog's teeth on a weekly basis. Start the dental-care routine while the Toller is still a puppy so that he will become accustomed to this type of handling.

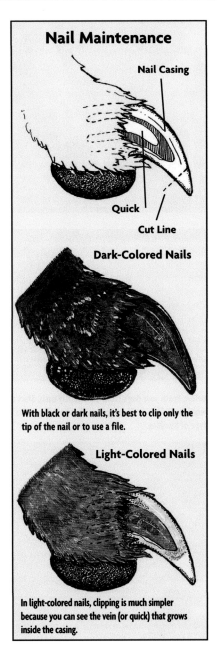

Nail Maintenance

Nail Casing

Quick

Cut Line

Dark-Colored Nails

With black or dark nails, it's best to clip only the tip of the nail or to use a file.

Light-Colored Nails

In light-colored nails, clipping is much simpler because you can see the vein (or quick) that grows inside the casing.

body—get all of the hard-to-reach places.

Once the dog has been thoroughly shampooed, he requires an equally thorough rinsing. Shampoo left in the coat can be irritating to the dog's skin. Protect his eyes from the shampoo by shielding them with your hand and directing the flow of water in the opposite direction. You also should avoid getting water in the ear canal. Be prepared for your dog to shake out his coat—you might want to stand back, but make sure you have a hold on the dog to keep him from running through the house. Have a heavy towel handy.

EAR CLEANING

The ears should be kept clean with a cotton ball and ear powder made especially for dogs. Do not probe into the ear canal with a cotton swab, as this can cause injury. Be on the lookout for any signs of infection or ear-mite infestation. If your Toller has been shaking his head or scratching at his ears frequently, this usually indicates a problem. If the dog's ears have an unusual odor, this is a sure sign of mite infestation or infection, and a signal to have his ears checked by the vet.

NAIL CLIPPING

Your Toller should be accustomed to having his nails trimmed at an early age since nail clipping will be part of your maintenance routine throughout his life. A dog's long nails can scratch someone unintentionally and also have a better chance of ripping and bleeding, or of causing the feet to spread. A good rule of thumb is that if you can hear your dog's nails' clicking on the floor when he walks, his nails are too long.

Before you start cutting, make sure you can identify the "quick" in each nail. The quick is a blood vessel that runs through the center of each nail and grows rather close to the end. The quick will bleed if accidentally cut, which will be quite painful for the dog as it contains nerve endings. Keep some type of clotting agent on hand, such as a styptic pencil or styptic powder (the type used for shaving). This will stop the bleeding quickly when applied to the end of the cut nail. Do not panic if you cut the quick, just stop the bleeding and talk soothingly to your dog. Once he has calmed down, move on to the next nail. It is better to clip a little at a time, particularly with black-nailed dogs.

Hold your pup steady as you begin trimming his nails; you do not want him to make any sudden movements or run away. Talk to him soothingly and stroke him as you clip. Holding his foot in your hand, simply take off the end of each nail with one swift clip. You should

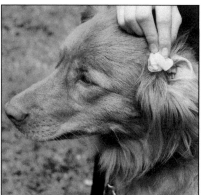

Clean the outer part of the ears with soft cotton and ear powder ● liquid. Never probe into the e● canal.

Clean gently around the eye area with a soft wipe and water ● special cleanser.

Below: Use a nail clipper made for dogs to maintain the proper length of your Toller's nails. Again, if you start with a young pup, he will grow up to tolerate having his nails clipped.

purchase nail clippers that are made for use on dogs; you can probably find them wherever you buy pet or grooming supplies. Some owners find those of the guillotine type easiest to use.

TRAVELING WITH YOUR DOG

CAR TRAVEL
You should accustom your Toller to riding in a car at an early age. You may or may not take him in the car often, but at the very least he will need to go to the vet and you do not want these trips to be traumatic for the dog or troublesome for you. The safest way for a dog to ride in the car is in a sturdy crate. If he is accustomed to using a crate in the house, he should have no problem with a travel crate.

Put the pup in the crate and see how he reacts. If he seems uneasy, you can have a passenger hold him on his lap while you drive. Another option for car travel is a specially made safety harness for dogs, which straps the dog in much like a seat belt. For those with large vehicles like sport utility vehicles, you can partition the back of the vehicle to create an area of safe confinement. Regardless of which option you choose, do not let the dog roam loose in the vehicle—this is very dangerous! If you should stop short, your dog can be thrown and injured. If the dog starts climbing on you and pestering you while you are driving, you will not be able to concentrate on the road. It is an unsafe situation for everyone—human and canine.

For long trips, be prepared to stop to let the dog relieve himself. Take with you whatever you need to clean up after him, including a "poop-scoop" and plastic bags, and some paper towels and perhaps some old bath towels for use should he have a potty accident in the car or suffer from motion sickness.

AIR TRAVEL
Contact your chosen airline before proceeding with your travel plans that include your Toller. The dog will be required to travel in a fiberglass crate and you should always check in advance with the airline regarding specific requirements for the crate's size, type and labeling. To

WATER, WATER EVERYWHERE
When you travel with your dog, it's a good idea to take along water from home or to buy bottled water for the trip. In areas where water is sometimes chemically treated and sometimes comes right out of the ground, you can prevent adverse reactions to this essential part of your dog's diet.

help put the dog at ease, give him one of his favorite toys in the crate. Do not feed the dog for several hours prior to checking in so that you minimize his need to relieve himself. However, some airlines require that the dog must be fed within a certain time frame of arriving at the airport, in which case a light meal is best. For long trips, you will have to attach food and water bowls to the dog's crate so that airline employees can tend to him between legs of the trip.

Make sure your dog is properly identified and that your contact information appears on his ID tags and on his crate. Your Toller will travel in a different area of the plane than the human passengers, so every rule must be strictly followed to prevent the risk of getting separated from your dog.

TRAVEL TIP

Never leave your dog alone in the car. In hot weather, your dog can die from the high temperature inside a closed vehicle; even a car parked in the shade can heat up very quickly. Leaving the window open is danger-ous as well since the dog can hurt himself trying to get out.

VACATIONS AND BOARDING

So you want to take a family vaca-tion—and you want to include *all* members of the family. You would probably make arrangements for accommodations ahead of time anyway, but this is especially important when traveling with a dog. You do not want to make an overnight stop at the only place around for miles, only to find out that they do not allow dogs. Also, you do not want to reserve a place

Visit several boarding kennels and have one in mind before you actually need its services. Be sure the dogs' quarters are clean and ample in size for your active Toller

for your family without confirming that you are traveling with a dog, because, if it is against their policy, you may end up without a place to stay.

Alternatively, if you are traveling and choose not to bring your Toller, you will have to make arrangements for him while you are away. Some options are to take him to a neighbor's house to stay while you are gone, to have a trusted neighbor stop by often or stay at your house or to bring your dog to a reputable boarding kennel. If you choose to board him at a kennel, you should visit in advance to see the facilities provided and where the dogs are kept. Are the dogs' areas spacious and kept clean? Talk to some of the employees and observe how they treat the dogs—do they spend time with the dogs, play with them, exercise them, etc.? Also find out the kennel's policy on vaccinations and what they require. This is for all of the dogs' safety, since there is a greater risk of diseases being passed from dog to dog when dogs are kept together.

COLLAR REQUIRED

If your dog gets lost, he is not able to ask for directions home. Identification tags fastened to the collar give important information—the dog's name, the owner's name, the owner's address and a telephone number where the owner can be reached. This makes it easy for whomever finds the dog to contact the owner and arrange to have the dog returned. An added advantage is that a person will be more likely to approach a lost dog who has ID tags on his collar; it tells the person that this is somebody's pet rather than a stray dog.

IDENTIFICATION

Your Nova Scotia Duck Tolling Retriever is your valued companion and friend. That is why you always keep a close eye on him and you have made sure that he cannot escape from the yard or wriggle out of his collar and run away from you. However, accidents can happen and there may come a time when your dog unexpectedly becomes separated from you. If this unfortunate event should occur, the first thing on your mind will be finding him. Proper identification, including an ID tag, and possibly a tattoo and/or a microchip, will increase the chances of his being returned to you safely and quickly.

This Toller has two important tags attached to his collar: his ID tag, giving important contact information, and a tag indicating that he has been microchipped for identification purposes.

TRAINING YOUR

NOVA SCOTIA
DUCK TOLLING RETRIEVER

Living with an untrained dog is a lot like owning a piano that you do not know how to play—it is a nice object to look at, but it does not do much more than that to bring you pleasure. Now try taking piano lessons, and suddenly the piano comes alive and brings forth magical sounds and rhythms that set your heart singing and your body swaying.

The same is true with your Toller. Any dog is a big responsibility and, if not trained sensibly, may develop unacceptable behavior that annoys you or could even cause family friction.

To train your Toller, you may like to enroll in an obedience class. Teach your dog good manners as you learn how and why he behaves the way he does. Find out how to communicate with your dog and how to recognize and understand his communications with you. Suddenly the dog takes on a new role in your life—he is clever, interesting, well behaved and fun to be with. He demonstrates his bond of devotion to you daily. In other words, your Toller does wonders for your ego because he constantly reminds

REAP THE REWARDS
If you start with a normal, healthy dog and give him time, patience and some carefully executed lessons, you will reap the rewards of that training for the life of the dog. And what a life it will be! The two of you will find immeasurable pleasure in the companionship you have nurtured together with love, respect and understanding.

you that you are not only his leader, you are his hero!

Those involved with teaching dog obedience and counseling owners about their dogs' behavior have discovered some interesting facts about dog ownership. For example, training dogs when they are puppies results in the highest rate of success in developing well-mannered and well-adjusted adult dogs. Training an older dog, from

When it comes to getting a curious pup's attention, nothing beats a treat!

PARENTAL GUIDANCE
Training a dog is a life experience. Many parents admit that much of what they know about raising children they learned from caring for their dogs. Dogs respond to love, fairness and guidance, just as children do. Become a good dog owner and you may become an even better parent.

six months to six years of age, can produce almost equal results, provided that the owner accepts the dog's slower rate of learning capability and is willing to work patiently to help the dog succeed at developing to his fullest potential. Unfortunately, many owners of untrained adult dogs lack the patience factor, so they do not persist until their dogs are successful at learning particular behaviors.

Training a puppy aged 10 to 16 weeks (20 weeks at the most) is like working with a dry sponge in a pool of water. The pup soaks up whatever you show him and constantly looks for more things to do and learn. At this early age, his body is not yet producing hormones, and therein lies the reason for such a high rate of success. Without hormones, he is focused on his owners and not particularly interested in investigating other places, dogs, people, etc. You are his leader: his provider of food, water, shelter and security. He latches onto you and wants to stay close. He will usually follow you from room to room, will not let you out of his sight when you are outdoors with him and will respond in like manner to the people and animals you encounter. If you greet a friend warmly, he will be happy to greet the person as well. If, however, you are hesitant or anxious about the approach of a stranger, he will respond according to how you act.

Once the puppy begins to produce hormones, his natural curiosity emerges and he begins to investigate the world around him. It is at this time when you may notice that the untrained dog begins to wander away from you and even ignore your commands to stay close. When this behavior becomes a problem, you have two choices: get rid of the dog or train him. It is strongly urged that you choose the latter option.

You usually will be able to find obedience classes within a reasonable distance from your

home, but you can also do a lot to train your dog yourself. Sometimes there are classes available, but the tuition is too costly. Whatever the circumstances, the solution to training your dog without formal obedience classes lies within the pages of this book.

This chapter is devoted to helping you train your Nova Scotia Duck Tolling Retriever at

He's more than just a dog, he's your friend! Nothing can beat the companionship of a well-trained Nova Scotia Duck Tolle

HONOR AND OBEY

Dogs are the most honorable animals in existence. They consider another species (humans) as their own. They interface with you. You are their leader. Puppies perceive children to be on their level; their actions around small children are different than their behavior around their adult masters.

MEALTIME

Mealtime should be a peaceful time for your puppy. Do not put his food and water bowls in a high-traffic area in the house. For example, give him his own little corner or area where he can eat undisturbed and where he will not be underfoot. Do not allow small children or other family members to disturb the pup when he is eating. He wants to enjoy his meal, too!

home. If the recommended procedures are followed faithfully, you may expect positive results that will prove rewarding both to you and your dog.

Whether your new charge is a puppy or a mature adult, the methods of teaching and the techniques we use in training basic behaviors are the same. After all, no dog, whether puppy or adult, likes harsh or inhumane methods. All creatures, however, respond favorably to gentle motivational methods and sincere praise and encouragement. Now let us get started.

HOUSE-TRAINING

You can train a puppy to relieve himself wherever you choose, but this must be somewhere suitable. You should bear in mind from the outset that when your puppy is old enough to go out in public places, any canine deposits must be removed at once. You will always have to carry with you a small plastic bag or "poop-scoop."

Outdoor training includes such surfaces as grass, soil and cement. Indoor training usually means training your dog to newspaper, not a viable option with a dog like the Toller. When deciding on the surface and location that you will want your Toller to use, be sure it is going to be permanent. Training your dog to grass and then changing your mind a few months later is extremely difficult for both dog and owner.

Next, choose the command you will use each and every time you want your puppy to void. "Hurry up" and "Let's go" are examples of commands commonly used by dog owners. Get in the habit of giving the puppy your chosen relief command before you take him out. That way, when he becomes an adult, you will be able to determine if he wants to go out when you ask him. A confirmation will be signs of interest such as wagging his tail, watching you intently, going to the door, etc.

PUPPY'S NEEDS

The puppy needs to relieve himself after play periods, after each meal, after he has been sleeping and at any time he indicates that he is looking for a place to urinate or defecate. The urinary and intestinal tract muscles of very young puppies are not fully developed. Therefore, like human babies, puppies need to relieve themselves frequently.

Take your puppy out often—every hour for an eight-week-old, for example—and always immediately after sleeping and eating. The older the puppy, the less often he will need to relieve himself. Finally, as a mature healthy adult, he will require only three to five relief trips per day.

HOUSING

Since the types of housing and control you provide for your puppy have a direct relationship on the success of house-training, we consider the various aspects of both before we begin training.

Taking a new puppy home and turning him loose in your house can be compared to turning a child loose in a sports arena and telling the child that the place is all his! The sheer enormity of the place would be too much for him to handle. Instead, offer the puppy clearly defined areas where he can play, sleep, eat and live. A room of the house where the family gathers is the most obvious choice. Puppies are social animals and need to feel a part of the pack right from the start. Hearing your voice, watching you while you are doing things and smelling you nearby are all positive reinforcers that he is now a member of your pack. Usually a family room, the kitchen or a nearby adjoining

HOW MANY TIMES A DAY?

AGE	RELIEF TRIPS
To 14 weeks	10
14–22 weeks	8
22–32 weeks	6
Adulthood	4
(dog stops growing)	

These are estimates, of course, but they are a guide to the *minimum* number of opportunities a dog should have each day to relieve himself.

CANINE DEVELOPMENT SCHEDULE

It is important to understand how and at what age a puppy develops into adulthood. If you are a puppy owner, consult the following Canine Development Schedule to determine the stage of development your puppy is currently experiencing. This knowledge will help you as you work with the puppy in the weeks and months ahead.

Period	Age	Characteristics
FIRST TO THIRD	BIRTH TO SEVEN WEEKS	The puppy needs food, sleep and warmth, and responds to simple and gentle touching. Needs mother for security and disciplining. Needs littermates for learning and interacting with other dogs. The pup learns to function within a pack and learns pack order of dominance. Begin socializing the pup with adults and children for short periods. The pup begins to become aware of his environment.
FOURTH	EIGHT TO TWELVE WEEKS	Brain is fully developed. Needs socializing with outside world. Remove from mother and littermates. Needs to change from canine pack to human pack. Human dominance necessary. Fear period occurs between 8 and 12 weeks. Avoid fright and pain.
FIFTH	THIRTEEN TO SIXTEEN WEEKS	Training and formal obedience should begin. Less association with other dogs, more with people, places, situations. Period will pass easily if you remember this is pup's change-to-adolescence time. Be firm and fair. Flight instinct prominent. Permissiveness and over-disciplining can do permanent damage. Praise for good behavior.
JUVENILE	FOUR TO EIGHT MONTHS	Another fear period about 7 to 8 months of age. It passes quickly, but be cautious of fright and pain. Sexual maturity reached. Dominant traits established. Dog should understand sit, down, come and stay by now.

NOTE: THESE ARE APPROXIMATE TIME FRAMES. ALLOW FOR INDIVIDUAL DIFFERENCES IN PUPPIES.

THINK BEFORE YOU BARK

Dogs are sensitive to their masters' moods and emotions. Use your voice wisely when communicating with your dog. Never raise your voice at your dog unless you are trying to correct him. "Barking" at your dog can become as meaningless as "dogspeak" is to you.

breakfast area is ideal for providing safety and security for both puppy and owner.

Within the designated room, there should be a smaller area that the puppy can call his own. An alcove, a wire or fiberglass dog crate or a fenced (not boarded!) corner from which he can view the activities of his new family will be fine. The size of the area or crate is the key factor here. The area must be large enough so that the puppy can lie down and stretch out, as well as stand up, without rubbing his head on the top. At the same time, it must be small enough so that he cannot relieve himself at one end and sleep at the other without coming into contact with his droppings before he is fully trained to relieve himself outside. Dogs are, by nature, clean animals and will not remain close to their relief areas unless forced to do so. In those cases, they then become dirty dogs and usually remain that way for life.

The dog's designated area should contain clean bedding and a toy. Water should always be available to your Toller, but avoid putting food or water in his crate until house-training is accomplished, as this will be counterproductive to your efforts.

CONTROL

By *control*, we mean helping the puppy to create a lifestyle pattern that will be compatible to that of his human pack (*you!*). Just as we guide little children to learn our

TAKE THE LEAD

Do not carry your dog to his relief area. Lead him there on a leash or, better yet, encourage him to follow you to the spot. If you start carrying him to his spot, you might end up doing this routine forever and your dog will have the satisfaction of having trained *you*.

COMMAND STANCE
Stand up straight and authoritatively when giving your dog commands. Do not issue commands when lying on the floor or lying on your back on the sofa. If you are on your hands and knees when you give a command, your dog will think you are positioning yourself to play.

way of life, we must show the puppy when it is time to play, eat, sleep, exercise and even entertain himself.

Your puppy should always sleep in his crate. He should also learn that, during times of household confusion and excessive human activity, such as at breakfast when family members are preparing for the day, he can play by himself in relative safety and comfort in his designated area. Each time you leave the puppy alone, he should understand exactly where he is to stay.

Puppies are chewers and cannot tell the difference between what is safe to chew on and lamp and television cords, shoes, table legs, etc. Chewing into a television wire, for example, can be fatal to the puppy, while a shorted wire can start a fire in the house. If the puppy chews on the arm of the chair when he is alone, you will probably discipline him angrily when you get home. Thus, he makes the association that your coming home means he is going to be punished. (He will not remember chewing the chair and is incapable of making the association of the discipline with his naughty deed.) Accustoming the pup to his designated area not only keeps him safe but also avoids his engaging in destructive behaviors when you are not around.

Times of excitement, such as special occasions, family parties,

THE CLEAN LIFE

By providing sleeping and resting quarters that fit the dog, and offering frequent opportunities to relieve himself outside his quarters, the puppy quickly learns that the outdoors is the place to go when he needs to urinate or defecate. It also reinforces his innate desire to keep his sleeping quarters clean. This, in turn, helps develop the muscle control that will eventually produce a dog with clean living habits.

Keep trips to his relief area short. Stay no more than five or six minutes and then return to the house. If he goes during that time, praise him lavishly and take him indoors immediately. If he does not, but he has an accident when you go back indoors, pick him up immediately, say "No! No!" and return to his relief area. Wait a few minutes, then return to the house again. Never hit a puppy or put his face in urine or excrement when he has had an accident!

Pups learn early lessons in cleanliness and behavior from their dam, and having a well behaved older dog in the home can help training, since pups take cues from adults and tend to follow their lead.

etc., can be fun for the puppy, provided that he can view the activities from the security of his designated area. He is not underfoot and he is not being fed all sorts of tidbits that will probably cause him stomach distress, yet he still feels a part of the fun.

ESTABLISHING A SCHEDULE
A puppy should be taken to his relief area each time he is released from his designated area, after meals, after play sessions and when he first awakens in the morning (at age eight weeks, this can mean 5 a.m.!). The puppy will indicate that he's ready "to go" by circling or sniffing busily—do not misinterpret these signs. For a puppy less than ten weeks of age, a routine of taking him out every hour is necessary. As the puppy grows, he will be able to wait for longer periods of time.

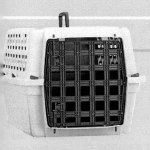

THE SUCCESS METHOD

Success that comes by luck is usually short-lived. Success that comes by well-thought-out proven methods is often more easily achieved and permanent. This is the Success Method. It is designed to give you, the puppy owner, a simple yet proven way to help your puppy develop clean living habits and a feeling of security in his new environment.

6 Steps to Successful Crate Training

1 Tell the puppy "Crate time!" and place him in the crate with a small treat (a piece of cheese or half of a biscuit). Let him stay in the crate for five minutes while you are in the same room. Then release him and praise lavishly. Never release him when he is fussing. Wait until he is quiet before you let him out.

2 Repeat Step 1 several times a day.

3 The next day, place the puppy in the crate as before. Let him stay there for ten minutes. Do this several times.

4 Continue building time in five-minute increments until the puppy stays in his crate for 30 minutes with you in the room. Always take him to his relief area after prolonged periods in his crate.

5 Now go back to Step 1 and let the puppy stay in his crate for five minutes, this time while you are out of the room.

6 Once again, build crate time in five-minute increments with you out of the room. When the puppy will stay willingly in his crate (he may even fall asleep!) for 30 minutes with you out of the room, he will be ready to stay in it for several hours at a time.

TRAINING RULES

If you want to be successful in training your dog, you have four rules to obey yourself:

1. Develop an understanding of how a dog thinks.
2. Do not blame the dog for lack of communication.
3. Define your dog's personality and act accordingly.
4. Have patience and be consistent.

Once indoors, put the puppy in his crate until you have had time to clean up his accident. Then, release him to the family area and watch him more closely than before. Chances are, his accident was a result of your not picking up his signal or waiting too long before offering him the opportunity to relieve himself. Never hold a grudge against the puppy for accidents.

Let the puppy learn that going outdoors means it is time to relieve himself, not to play. Once trained, he will be able to play indoors and out and still differentiate between the times for play versus the times for relief. Help him develop regular hours for naps, being alone, playing by himself and just resting, all in his crate. Encourage him to entertain himself while you are busy with your activities. Let him learn that having you near is comforting, but it is not your main purpose in life to provide him with undivided attention. Each time you put your puppy in his own area, use the same command, whatever suits best. Soon he will run to his crate or special area when he hears you say those words.

Crate training provides safety for you, the puppy and the home. It also provides the puppy with a feeling of security, and that helps the puppy achieve self-confidence and clean habits. Remember that one of the primary ingredients in

One of the rewards of training is the fun you can have with your Toller in different activities. This young lady and her dog are practicing "freestyle," a type of competition in which dogs and owners perform dance routines and are judged against other pairs.

house-training your puppy is control. Regardless of your lifestyle, there will always be occasions when you will need to have a place where your dog can stay and be happy and safe. Crate training is the answer for now and in the future.

In conclusion, a few key elements are really all you need for a successful house-training method—consistency, frequency, praise, control and supervision. By following these procedures with a normal, healthy puppy, you and the puppy will soon be past the stage of "accidents" and ready to move on to a full and rewarding life together.

ROLES OF DISCIPLINE, REWARD AND PUNISHMENT

Discipline, training one to act in accordance with rules, brings order to life. It is as simple as that. Without discipline, particularly in a group society, chaos will reign supreme and the group will eventually perish. Humans and canines are social animals and need some form of discipline in order to function effectively. They must procure food, reproduce to keep their species going and protect their home base and their young. If there were no discipline in the lives of social animals, they would eventually die from starvation and/or predation by other stronger animals. In the case of domestic canines, discipline in their lives is needed in order for them to understand how their pack (you and other family members) functions and how they must act in order to survive.

A large humane society in a highly populated area recently surveyed dog owners regarding their satisfaction with their relationships with their dogs. People who had trained their dogs were

FAMILY TIES

If you have other pets in the home and/or interact often with the pets of friends and other family members, your dog will respond to those pets in much the same manner as you do. It is only when you show fear of or resentment toward another animal that he will act fearful or unfriendly.

75% more satisfied with their pets than those who had never trained their dogs.

Dr. Edward Thorndike, a well-known psychologist, established *Thorndike's Theory of Learning*, which states that a behavior that results in a pleasant event tends to be repeated. Furthermore, it concludes that a behavior that results in an unpleasant event tends not to be repeated. It is this theory upon which training methods are based today. For example, if you manipulate a dog to perform a specific behavior and reward him for doing it, he is likely to do it again because he enjoyed the end result.

Occasionally, punishment, a penalty inflicted for an offense, is necessary. The best type of punishment often comes from an outside source. For example, a

Multiple Tollers mean exponential patience and effort in training to keep the dogs safe and under control.

child is told not to touch the stove because he may get burned. He disobeys and touches the stove. In doing so, he receives a burn. From that time on, he respects the heat of the stove and avoids contact with it. Therefore, a behavior that results in an unpleasant event tends not to be repeated.

A good example of a dog's learning the hard way is the dog who chases the house cat. He is told many times to leave the cat alone, yet he persists in teasing the cat. Then, one day, the dog begins chasing the cat and the cat turns and swipes a claw across the dog's face, leaving the dog with a painful gash on his nose. The final result is that the dog stops chasing the cat.

LANGUAGE BARRIER

Dogs do not understand our language and have to rely on tone of voice more than just works or sound. They can be trained to react to a certain sound, at a certain volume. If you say "No, Oliver" in a very soft, pleasant voice, it will not have the same meaning as "No, Oliver!!" when you raise your voice. You should never use the dog's name during a reprimand, just the command "No! " You never want the dog to associate his name with a negative experience or reprimand.

The intelligent Toller makes an attentive and capable student when lessons are kept upbeat, positive and interesting.

THE STUDENT'S STRESS TEST

During training sessions, you must be able to recognize signs of stress in your dog, such as:

• tucking his tail between his legs
• lowering his head
• shivering or trembling
• standing completely still or running away
• panting and/or salivating
• avoiding eye contact
• flattening his ears back
• urinating submissively
• rolling over and lifting a leg
• grinning or baring teeth
• aggression when restrained

If your four-legged student displays these signs, he may just be nervous or intimidated. The training session may have been too lengthy, with not enough praise and affirmation. Stop for the day and try again tomorrow.

TRAINING EQUIPMENT

COLLAR AND LEAD

For a Toller, the collar and lead that you use for training must be one with which you are easily able to work, not too heavy for the dog and perfectly safe.

TREATS

Have a bag of treats on hand; something nutritious and easy to swallow works best. Use a soft treat, a chunk of cheese or a piece of cooked chicken rather than a dry biscuit. By the time the dog has finished chewing a dry treat, he will forget why he is being rewarded in the first place!

Using food rewards will not teach a dog to beg at the table—the only way to teach a dog to beg at the table is to give him food from the table. In training, rewarding the dog with a food treat will help him associate praise and the treats with learning new behaviors that obviously please his owner.

KEEP SMILING
Never train your dog, puppy or adult, when you are angry or in a sour mood. Dogs are very sensitive to human feelings, especially anger, and if your dog senses that you are angry or upset, he will connect your anger with his training and learn to resent or fear his training sessions.

TRAINING BEGINS:
ASK THE DOG A QUESTION

In order to teach your dog anything, you must first get his attention. After all, he cannot learn anything if he is looking away from you with his mind on something else.

To get your dog's attention, ask him "School?" and immediately walk over to him and give him a treat as you tell him "Good dog." Wait a minute or two and repeat the routine, this time with a treat in your hand as you approach within a foot of the dog. Do not go directly to him, but stop about a foot short of him and hold out the treat as you ask "School?" He will see you approaching with a treat in your hand and most likely begin walking toward you. As you meet, give him the treat and praise again.

The third time, ask the question, have a treat in your hand and walk only a short distance toward the dog so that he must walk almost all the way to you.

As he reaches you, give him the treat and praise again.

By this time, the dog will probably be getting the idea that if he pays attention to you, especially when you ask that question, it will pay off in treats and enjoyable activities for him. In other words, he learns that "school" means doing great things with you that are fun and that result in positive attention for him.

Remember that the dog does not understand your verbal language; he only recognizes sounds. Your question translates to a series of sounds for him, and those sounds become the signal to go to you and pay attention. The dog learns that if he does this, he will get to interact with you plus receive treats and praise.

The sit command is a basic and easily taught exercise. Sometimes the dog needs a little "push" on his rea to show what's expected of him.

THE BASIC COMMANDS

TEACHING SIT

Now that you have the dog's attention, attach his lead and hold it in your left hand, and hold a food treat in your right hand. Place your food hand at the dog's nose and let him lick the treat but not take it from you. Say "Sit" and slowly raise your food hand from in front of the dog's nose up over his head so that he is looking at the ceiling. As he bends his head upward, he will have to bend his knees to maintain his balance. As he bends his knees, he will assume a sit position. At that point, release the food treat

and praise lavishly with comments such as "Good dog! Good sit!," etc. Remember to always praise enthusiastically, because dogs relish verbal praise from their owners and feel so proud of themselves whenever they accomplish a behavior.

You will not use food forever in getting the dog to obey your commands. Food is only used to teach new behaviors and, once the dog knows what you want when you give a specific command, you will wean him off the food treats but still maintain the verbal praise. After all, you will always have your voice with you, and there will be many times when you have no food rewards but expect the dog to obey.

TEACHING DOWN

Teaching the down exercise is easy when you understand how the dog perceives the down position, and it is very difficult when you do not. Dogs perceive the down position as a submissive one; therefore, teaching the down exercise by using a forceful method can sometimes make the dog develop such a fear of the down that he either runs away when you say "Down" or he attempts to snap at the person who tries to force him down.

Have the dog sit alongside your left leg, facing in the same direction as you are. Hold the lead in your left hand and a

DOUBLE JEOPARDY

A dog in jeopardy never lies down. He stays alert on his feet because instinct tells him that he may have to run away or fight for his survival. Therefore, if a dog feels threatened or anxious, he will not lie down. Consequently, it is important to keep the dog calm and relaxed as he learns the down exercise.

food treat in your right. Now place your left hand lightly on the top of the dog's shoulders where they meet above the spinal cord. Do not push down on the dog's shoulders; simply rest your left hand there so you can guide the dog to lie down close to your left leg rather than to swing away from your side when he drops.

Now place the food hand at the dog's nose, say "Down" very softly (almost a whisper) and slowly lower the food hand to the dog's front feet. When the food hand reaches the floor, begin

CONSISTENCY PAYS OFF

Dogs need consistency in their feeding schedule, exercise and relief visits, and in the verbal commands you use. If you use "Stay" on Monday and "Stay here, please" on Tuesday, you will confuse your dog. Don't demand perfect behavior during training sessions and then let him have the run of the house the rest of the day. Above all, lavish praise on your pet consistently every time he does something right. The more he feels he is pleasing you, the more willing he will be to learn.

The sit/stay is a natural progression once the original exercise has been mastered.

moving it forward along the floor in front of the dog. Keep talking softly to the dog, saying things like, "Do you want this treat? You can do this, good dog." Your reassuring tone of voice will help calm the dog as he tries to follow the food hand in order to get the treat.

When the dog's elbows touch the floor, release the food and praise softly. Try to get the dog to maintain that down position for several seconds before you let him sit up again. The goal here is to get the dog settled and not feeling threatened in the down position.

TEACHING STAY

It is easy to teach the dog to stay in either a sit or a down position. Again, we use food and praise during the teaching process as we help the dog to understand exactly what it is that we are expecting him to do.

To teach the sit/stay, start with the dog sitting on your left side as before and hold the lead in your left hand. Have a food treat in your right hand and place your

For your puppy's safety, teaching him to come when called is perhaps the most important exercise.

> **"COME" . . . BACK**
> Never call your dog to come to you for a correction or scold him when he reaches you. That is the quickest way to turn a "Come" command into "Go away fast!" Dogs think only in the present tense, and your dog will connect the scolding with coming to you, not with the misbehavior of a few moments earlier.

food hand at the dog's nose. Say "Stay" and step out on your right foot to stand directly in front of the dog, toe to toe, as he licks and nibbles the treat. Be sure to keep his head facing upward to maintain the sit position. Count to five and then swing around to stand next to the dog again with him on your left. As soon as you get back to the original position, release the food and praise lavishly.

To teach the down/stay, do the down as previously described. As soon as the dog lies down, say "Stay" and step out on your right foot just as you did in the sit/stay. Count to five and then return to stand beside the dog with him on your left side. Release the treat and praise as always.

Within a week or ten days, you can begin to add a bit of distance between you and your dog when you leave him. When you do, use your left hand open with the palm facing the dog as a stay signal, much the same as the

THE GOLDEN RULE

The golden rule of dog training is simple. For each "question" (command), there is only one correct answer (reaction). One command = one reaction. Keep practicing the command until the dog reacts correctly without hesitating. Be repetitive but not monotonous. Dogs get bored just as people do!

hand signal a police officer uses to stop traffic at an intersection. Hold the food treat in your right hand as before, but this time the food will not be touching the dog's nose. He will watch the food hand and quickly learn that he is going to get that treat as soon as you return to his side.

When you can stand 3 feet away from your dog for 30 seconds, you can then begin building time and distance in both stays. Eventually, the dog can be expected to remain in the stay position for prolonged periods of time until you return to him or call him to you. Always praise lavishly when he stays.

TEACHING COME

If you make teaching "come" an exciting experience, you should never have a student that does not love the game or that fails to come when called. The secret, it seems, is never to teach the word "come."

At times when an owner most wants his dog to come when called, the owner is likely to be upset or anxious and he allows these feelings to come through in the tone of his voice when he calls his dog. Hearing that desperation in his owner's voice, the dog fears the results of going to him and therefore either disobeys outright or runs in the opposite direction. The secret, therefore, is to teach the dog a game and, when you want him to come to you, simply play the game. It is practically a no-fail solution!

To begin, have several members of your family take a few food treats and each go into a different room in the house. Everyone takes turns calling the dog, and each person should celebrate the dog's finding him with a treat and lots of happy praise.

The stay exercise shown here in the down position, can be reinforced with a hand signal in addition to the voice command.

When a person calls the dog, he is actually inviting the dog to find him and to get a treat as a reward for "winning."

A few turns of the "Where are you?" game and the dog will understand that everyone is playing the game and that each person has a big celebration awaiting the dog's success at locating him or her. Once the dog learns to love the game, simply calling out "Where are you?" will bring him running to you from wherever he is when he hears that all-important question.

The come command is recognized as one of the most important things to teach a dog, but there are trainers who work with thousands of dogs and never use the actual word "come." Yet these dogs will race to respond to a person who uses the dog's name followed by "Where are you?" For example, a woman has a 12-year-old companion dog who went blind, but who never fails to locate her owner when asked, "Where are you?"

Whether a leisurely stroll, brisk walk or jog, heeling means that the dog stays by his owner's side, at his owner's pace.

FEAR AGGRESSION

Pups who are subjected to physical abuse during training commonly end up with behavioral problems as adults. One common result of abuse is fear aggression, in which a dog will lash out, bare his teeth, snarl and finally bite someone by whom he feels threatened. For example, your daughter may be playing with the dog one afternoon. As they play hide-and-seek, she backs the dog into a corner and, as she attempts to tease him playfully, he bites her hand. Examine the cause of this behavior. Did your daughter ever hit the dog? Did someone who resembles your daughter hit or scream at the dog?

Fortunately, fear aggression is relatively easy to correct. Have your daughter engage in only positive activities with the dog, such as feeding, petting and walking. She should not give any corrections or negative feedback. If the dog still growls or cowers away from her, allow someone else to accompany them. After approximately one week, the dog should feel that he can rely on her for many positive things, and he will also be prevented from reacting fearfully towards anyone who might resemble her.

Children, in particular, love to play this game with their dogs. Children can hide in smaller places like a shower or bathtub, behind a bed or under a table. The dog needs to work a little bit harder to find these hiding places, but, when he does, he loves to celebrate with a treat and a tussle with a favorite youngster.

TEACHING HEEL

Heeling means that the dog walks beside the owner without pulling. It takes time and patience on the owner's part to succeed at teaching the dog that he (the owner) will not proceed unless the dog is walking calmly beside him. Neither pulling out ahead on the lead nor lagging behind is acceptable.

Begin by holding the lead in your left hand as the dog sits beside your left leg. Move the loop end of the lead to your right hand, but keep your left hand short on the lead so that it keeps the dog in close next to you.

Say "Heel" and step forward on your left foot. Keep the dog close to you and take three steps. Stop and have the dog sit next to you in what we now call the heel position. Praise verbally, but do not touch the dog. Hesitate a moment and begin again with "Heel," taking three steps and stopping, at which point the dog is told to sit again.

Your goal here is to have the dog walk those three steps with-

SAFETY FIRST

While it may seem that the most important things to your dog are eating, sleeping and chewing the upholstery on your furniture, his first concern is actually safety. The domesticated dogs we keep as companions have the same pack instinct as their ancestors who ran free thousands of years ago. Because of this pack instinct, your dog wants to know that he and his pack are not in danger of being harmed, and that his pack has a strong, capable leader. You must establish yourself as the leader early on in your relationship. That way your dog will trust that you will take care of him and the pack, and he will accept your commands without question.

Daily walks should be a part of your Toller's exercise, making polite on-lead behavior a necessity.

A good-looking, well-behaved family bunch. On the far right is the dam, pictured with her offspring from two different litters. From left to right: a 20-month-old male; two 20-month-old females; two five-year-old males; and the proud mother.

out pulling on the lead. Once he will walk calmly beside you for three steps without pulling, increase the number of steps you take to five. When he will walk politely beside you while you take five steps, you can increase the length of your walk to ten steps. Keep increasing the length of your stroll until the dog will walk quietly beside you without pulling as long as you want him to heel. When you stop heeling, indicate to the dog that the exercise is over by verbally praising as you pet him and say "OK, good dog." The "OK" is used as a release word, meaning that the exercise is finished and the dog is free to relax.

If you are dealing with a dog who insists on pulling you around, simply "put on your brakes" and stand your ground until the dog realizes that the two of you are not going anywhere until he is beside you and moving at your pace, not his. It may take some time just standing there to convince the dog that you are the leader and that you will be the one to decide on the direction and speed of your travel.

Each time the dog looks up at you or slows down to give a slack lead between the two of you,

OBEDIENCE SCHOOL
Taking your dog to an obedience school may be the best investment in time and money you can ever make. You will enjoy the benefits for the lifetime of your dog and you will have the opportunity to meet people who have similar expectations for their companion dogs.

quietly praise him and say, "Good heel. Good dog." Eventually, the dog will begin to respond and within a few days he will be walking politely beside you without pulling on the lead. At first, the training sessions should be kept short and very positive; soon the dog will be able to walk nicely with you for increasingly longer distances. Remember also to give the dog free time and the opportunity to run and play when you have finished heel practice.

WEANING OFF FOOD IN TRAINING
Food is used in training new behaviors. Once the dog understands what behavior goes with a specific command, it is time to start weaning him off the food treats. At first, give a treat after each exercise. Then, start to give a treat only after every other exercise. Mix up the times when you offer a food reward and the times when you only offer praise so that the dog will never know

when he is going to receive both food and praise and when he is going to receive only praise. This is called a variable ratio reward system. It proves successful because there is always the chance that the owner will produce a treat, so the dog never stops trying for that reward. No matter what, *always* give verbal praise.

OBEDIENCE CLASSES
It is a good idea to enroll in an obedience class if one is available in your area. If yours is a show dog, handling classes would be more appropriate. Many areas have dog clubs that offer basic obedience training as well as preparatory classes for obedience competition. There are also local dog trainers who offer similar classes. The highly trainable Toller usually enjoys obedience training as long as the lessons are kept short and interesting.

At obedience trials, dogs can earn titles at various levels of competition. The beginning levels of obedience competition include basic behaviors such as sit, down, heel, etc. The more advanced levels of competition include jumping, retrieving, scent discrimination and signal work. The advanced levels require a dog and owner to put a lot of time and effort into their training. The titles that can be earned at these levels of competition are very prestigious.

Training to retrieve in water starts with showing the Toller the object to retrieve, sparking his interest.

The Toller races after the ball thrown into the water.

He leaps into the water with energy and excitement.

Still getting the hang of swimming, the Toller splashes happily toward his goal.

Almost there...

Success! Swimming back to his master, with the ball securely in his mouth.

There is no Toller happier than one who can do what he loves...whether in actual hunting or in training for and participating in hunting and instinct tests.

OTHER ACTIVITIES FOR LIFE

Whether a dog is trained in the structured environment of a class or alone with his owner at home, there are many activities that can bring fun and rewards to both owner and dog once they have mastered basic control.

Teaching the dog to help out around the home, in the garden or on the farm provides great satisfaction to both dog and owner. In addition, the dog's help makes life a little easier for his owner and raises his stature as a valued companion to his family. It helps give the dog a purpose by occupying his mind and providing an outlet for his energy.

Backpacking is an exciting and healthy activity that the dog can be taught without assistance from more than his owner. The exercise of walking and climbing is good for man and dog alike, and the bond that they develop together is priceless. The rule for backpacking with any dog is never to expect the dog to carry more than one-sixth of his body weight.

Of course, if you wish to utilize your Toller's natural skills and instincts, the breed excels at hunting waterfowl and is also used successfully on upland game. If you are interested in participating in organized competition with your Toller, there are activities other than obedience in which you and your dog can become involved. Tollers are fairly independent thinkers in the field, so few excel in field trials, which requires structured and more rigid training. They are eligible to compete in retriever field trials, although that is extremely rare. Hunting tests set up to test field and obedience skills are more suitable for the Toller.

Agility is a popular sport in which dogs run through obstacle courses that include various jumps, tunnels and other exercises to test the dog's speed and coordination. Training for agility can begin when the dog is 12 months old or older. The agile Toller does very well in agility competiton. During the agility trial, the owners run beside their dogs to give commands and to guide them through the course. Although competitive, the focus is on fun—it's fun to do, fun to watch and great exercise.

AMERICAN KENNEL CLUB TITLES

The AKC offers over 40 different titles to dogs in competition. Depending on the events that your dog can enter, different titles apply. Some titles can be applied as prefixes, meaning that they are placed before the dog's name (e.g., Ch. King of the Road) and others are used as suffixes, placed after the dog's name (e.g., King of the Road, CD).

These titles are used as prefixes:

Conformation Dog Shows
- Ch. (Champion)

Obedience Trials
- NOC (National Obedience Champion)
- OTCH (Obedience Trial Champion)
- VCCH (Versatile Companion Champion)

Tracking Tests
- CT (Champion Tracker (TD,TDX and VST)

Agility Trials
- MACH (Master Agility Champion)
- MACH2, MACH3, MACH4, etc. . .

Field Trials
- FC (Field Champion)
- AFC (Amateur Field Champion)
- NFC (National Field Champion)
- NAFC (National Amateur Field Champion)
- NOGDC (National Open Gun Dog Champion)
- AKC GDSC (AKC Gun Dog Stake Champion)
- AKC RGDSC (AKC Retrieving Gun Dog Stake Champion)

Herding Trials
- HC (Herding Champion)

Dual
- DC (Dual Champion — Ch. and FC)

Triple
- TC (Triple Champion — Ch., FC and OTCH)

Coonhounds
- NCH (Nite Champion)
- GNCH (Grand Nite Champion)
- SHNCH (Senior Grand Nite Champion)
- GCH (Senior Champion)
- SGCH (Senior Grand Champion)
- GFC (Grand Field Champion)
- SGFC (Senior Grand Field Champion)
- WCH (Water Race Champion)
- GWCH (Water Race Grand Champion)
- SGWCH (Senior Grand Water Race Champion)

These titles are used as suffixes:

Obedience
- CD (Companion Dog)
- CDX (Companion Dog Excellent)
- UD (Utility Dog)
- UDX (Utility Dog Excellent)
- VCD1 (Versatile Companion Dog 1)
- VCD2 (Versatile Companion Dog 2)
- VCD3 (Versatile Companion Dog 3)
- VCD4 (Versatile Companion Dog 4)

Tracking Tests
- TD (Tracking Dog)
- TDX (Tracking Dog Excellent)
- VST (Variable Surface Tracker)

Agility Trials
- NA (Novice Agility)
- OA (Open Agility)
- AX (Agility Excellent)
- MX (Master Agility Excellent)
- NAJ (Novice Jumpers with weaves)
- OAJ (Open Jumpers with weaves)
- AXJ (Excellent Jumpers with weaves)
- MXJ (Master Excellent Jumpers with weaves)

Hunting Test
- JH (Junior Hunter)
- SH (Senior Hunter)
- MH (Master Hunter)

Herding Test
- HT (Herding Tested)
- PT (Pre-Trial Tested)
- HS (Herding Started)
- HI (Herding Intermediate)
- HX (Herding Excellent)

Lure Coursing
- JC (Junior Courser)
- SC (Senior Courser)
- MC (Master Courser)

Earthdog
- JE (Junior Earthdog)
- SE (Senior Earthdog)
- ME (Master Earthdog)

Lure Coursing
- JC (Junior Courser)
- SC (Senior Courser)
- MC (Master Courser)

Training for agility: The handler throws a ball over the hurdle to encourage the Toller to jump the hurdle to fetch the ball.

Tollers are eager learners and very agile...and they love to retrieve.

Training your Toller to retrieve usually starts in a spacious but secure area, using a dummy or bumper.

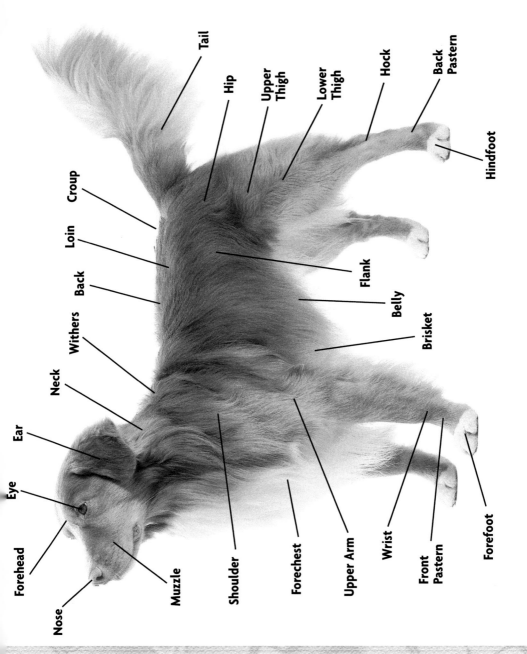

PHYSICAL STRUCTURE OF THE NOVA SCOTIA DUCK TOLLING RETRIEVER

NOVA SCOTIA
DUCK TOLLING RETRIEVER

Dogs suffer from many of the same physical illnesses as people and might even share many of the same psychological problems. Since people usually know more about human diseases than canine maladies, many of the terms used in this chapter will be familiar but not necessarily those used by vets. For example, we will use the familiar term *x-ray* instead of *radiograph*. We will also use the familiar term *symptoms*, even though dogs don't have symptoms, which are verbal descriptions of something the patient feels or observes himself that he regards as abnormal. Dogs have *clinical signs* since they cannot speak, so we have to look for these clinical signs…but we still use the term *symptoms* in the book.

Medicine is a constantly changing art, with some scientific input as well. Things alter as we learn more and more about basic sciences such as genetics and biochemistry, and have use of more sophisticated imaging techniques like Computer Aided Tomography (CAT scans) or Magnetic Resonance Imaging (MRI scans). There is academic dispute about many canine maladies, so different vets treat them in different ways, and some vets place a greater emphasis on surgical techniques than others.

SELECTING A QUALIFIED VET

Your selection of a vet should be based on personal recommendation for his skills with small animals, especially dogs, and, if possible, especially retriever breeds. If the vet is based nearby, it will be helpful because you might have an emergency or need to make multiple visits for treatments.

All vets are licensed and capable of dealing with routine medical issues such as infections, injuries and the promotion of health (for example, by vaccination). If the problem affecting your dog is more complex, your vet should refer your pet to someone with a more detailed knowledge of what is wrong. This will usually be a specialist who concentrates on a specific field, i.e., veterinary dermatology, veterinary ophthalmology, etc; whatever is the relevant field.

Veterinary procedures are very costly and as the treatments avail-

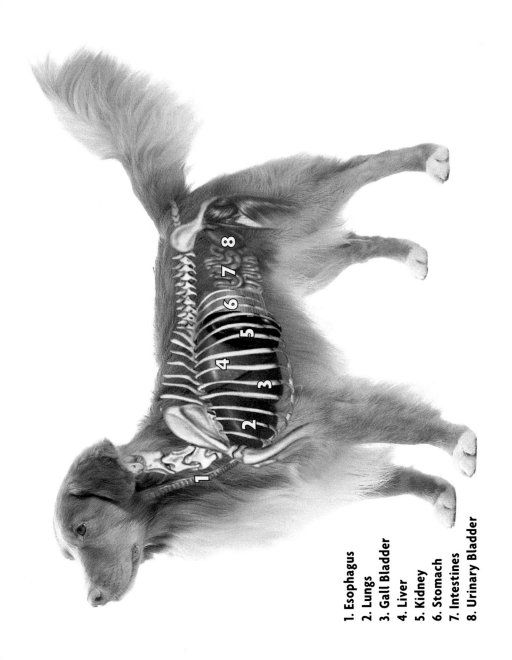

1. Esophagus
2. Lungs
3. Gall Bladder
4. Liver
5. Kidney
6. Stomach
7. Intestines
8. Urinary Bladder

INTERNAL ORGANS OF THE NOVA SCOTIA DUCK TOLLING RETRIEVER

able improve, they become more expensive. It is quite acceptable to discuss matters of cost with your vet; if there is more than one treatment option, cost may be a factor in deciding which route to take.

Insurance against veterinary cost is also becoming very popular. This may not pay for routine vaccinations, but will cover the costs for unexpected emergencies such as emergency surgery if, for example, the dog should be struck by a car.

PREVENTATIVE MEDICINE
It is much easier, less costly and more effective to practice preventative medicine than to fight bouts of illness and disease. Properly bred puppies of all breeds come from parents that were selected based upon their genetic disease profiles. The puppies' mother should have been vaccinated, free of all internal and external parasites and properly nourished. For these reasons, a visit to the vet who cared for the dam is recommended if at all possible. The dam passes disease resistance to her puppies, which should last from eight to ten weeks. Unfortunately, she can also pass on parasites and infection. This is why knowledge about her health is useful in learning more about the health of the puppies.

WEANING TO FIVE MONTHS OLD
Puppies should be weaned by the time they are two months old. A puppy that remains for at least

eight weeks with his mother and littermates usually adapts better to other dogs and people later in life.

Sometimes new owners have their puppy examined by a vet immediately, which is a good idea unless the puppy is overtired by a long journey. If this is the case, the pup should visit the vet within the first couple of days of leaving the breeder.

The puppy will have his teeth examined and have his skeletal conformation and general health checked prior to certification by the vet. Puppies in certain breeds have problems with their kneecaps, cataracts and other eye problems, heart murmurs and undescended testicles. Your vet also might have training in temperament evaluation. At the first visit, the vet will set up a vaccination schedule for the pup.

VACCINATIONS
Most vaccinations are given by injection and should only be given by a vet. Both he and you should keep a record of the date of the injection, the identification of the vaccine and the amount given. Some vets give a first vaccination at eight weeks, but most dog breeders prefer the course not to commence until about ten weeks because of the risk of interaction with the antibodies produced by the mother. The vaccination schedule is usually based on a 15-day cycle. You must take your vet's

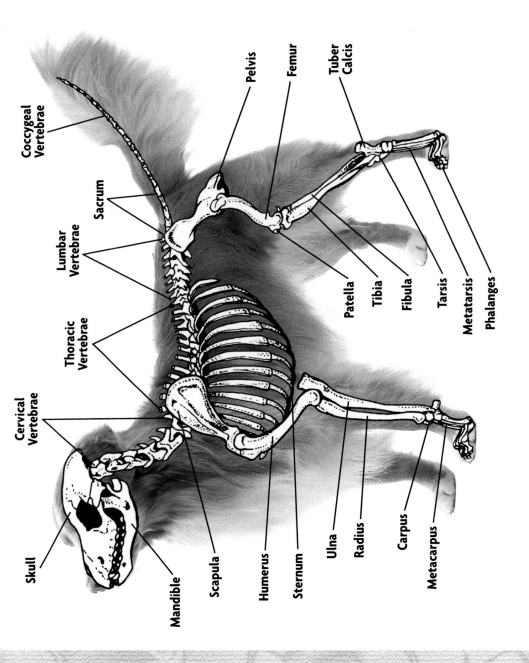

SKELETAL STRUCTURE OF THE NOVA SCOTIA DUCK TOLLING RETRIEVER

MORE THAN VACCINES

Vaccinations help prevent your new puppy from contracting diseases, but they do not cure them. Proper nutrition as well as parasite control keep your dog healthy and less susceptible to many dangerous diseases. Remember that your dog depends on you to ensure his well-being.

advice as to when to vaccinate, as this may differ according to the vaccine used.

The usual vaccines contain immunizing doses of several different viruses such as distemper, parvovirus, parainfluenza and hepatitis. There are other vaccines available when the puppy is at risk. You should rely upon professional advice. This is especially true for the booster immunizations. Most vaccination programs require a booster when the puppy is a year old and once a year thereafter. In some cases, circumstances may require more or less frequent immunizations.

Kennel cough, more formally known as tracheobronchitis, is immunized against with a vaccine that is sprayed into the dog's nostrils. Kennel cough is usually included in routine vaccination, but it is often not as effective as the vaccines for other major diseases.

HEALTH AND VACCINATION SCHEDULE

Age in Weeks:	6th	8th	10th	12th	14th	16th	20-24th	52nd
Worm Control	✔	✔	✔	✔	✔	✔	✔	
Neutering								✔
Heartworm		✔		✔		✔	✔	
Parvovirus	✔		✔		✔		✔	✔
Distemper		✔		✔		✔		✔
Hepatitis		✔		✔		✔		✔
Leptospirosis								✔
Parainfluenza	✔		✔		✔			✔
Dental Examination		✔					✔	✔
Complete Physical		✔					✔	✔
Coronavirus				✔			✔	✔
Kennel Cough	✔							
Hip Dysplasia								✔
Rabies							✔	

Vaccinations are not instantly effective. It takes about two weeks for the dog's immune system to develop antibodies. Most vaccinations require annual booster shots. Your vet should guide you in this regard.

FIVE MONTHS TO ONE YEAR OF AGE
Unless you intend to breed or show your dog, neutering the puppy at around six months of age is recommended; discuss this with your vet. A reputable breeder sells pups on the condition that any pups not intended for or of insufficient quality for breeding/showing be neutered. Neutering/spaying has proven to be extremely beneficial to male and female puppies, respectively. Besides eliminating the possibility of pregnancy, it inhibits (but does not prevent) breast cancer in bitches and prostate cancer in male dogs. Discuss the best time to neuter or spay with your vet.

Your vet should provide your puppy with a thorough dental evaluation at six months of age, ascertaining whether all of the permanent teeth have erupted properly. A home dental-care regimen should be initiated at six months, including brushing weekly and providing good dental devices (such as hard plastic or nylon bones). Regular dental care promotes healthy teeth, fresh breath and a longer life.

DOGS OLDER THAN ONE YEAR
Continue to visit the vet at least once a year. There is no such disease as "old age," but bodily functions do change with age. The eyes and ears are no longer as efficient. Liver, kidney and intestinal functions often decline.

Proper dietary changes, recommended by your vet, can make life more pleasant for your aging Toller and you.

SKIN PROBLEMS
Vets are consulted by dog owners for skin problems more than for any other group of diseases or maladies. A dog's skin is as sensitive, if not more so, than human skin, and both suffer almost the same ailments (though the occurrence of acne in most breeds is rare!). For this reason, veterinary dermatology has developed into a specialty practiced by many vets.

Since many skin problems have visual symptoms that are almost identical, it requires the skill of an experienced veterinary dermatologist to identify and cure many of the more severe skin disorders. Pet shops sell many treatments for skin problems, but most of the treatments are directed at symptoms and not at the underlying problem(s). If your dog is suffering from a skin disorder, you should seek professional assistance as quickly as possible. As with all diseases, the earlier a problem is identified and treated, the more likely that the cure will work.

HEREDITARY SKIN DISORDERS
Veterinary dermatologists are currently researching a number of skin disorders that are believed to have a hereditary basis. These

DISEASE REFERENCE CHART

	What is it?	What causes it?	Symptoms
Leptospirosis	Severe disease that affects the internal organs; can be spread to people.	A bacterium, which is often carried by rodents, that enters through mucous membranes and spreads quickly throughout the body.	Range from fever, vomiting and loss of appetite in less severe cases to shock, irreversible kidney damage and possibly death in most severe cases.
Rabies	Potentially deadly virus that infects warm-blooded mammals.	Bite from a carrier of the virus, mainly wild animals.	1st stage: dog exhibits change in behavior, fear. 2nd stage: dog's behavior becomes more aggressive. 3rd stage: loss of coordination, trouble with bodily functions.
Parvovirus	Highly contagious virus, potentially deadly.	Ingestion of the virus, which is usually spread through the feces of infected dogs.	Most common: severe diarrhea. Also vomiting, fatigue, lack of appetite.
Kennel cough	Contagious respiratory infection.	Combination of types of bacteria and virus. Most common: *Bordetella bronchiseptica* bacteria and parainfluenza virus.	Chronic cough.
Distemper	Disease primarily affecting respiratory and nervous system.	Virus that is related to the human measles virus.	Mild symptoms such as fever, lack of appetite and mucous secretion progress to evidence of brain damage, "hard pad."
Hepatitis	Virus primarily affecting the liver.	Canine adenovirus type I (CAV-1). Enters system when dog breathes in particles.	Lesser symptoms include listlessness, diarrhea, vomiting. More severe symptoms include "blue-eye" (clumps of virus in eye).
Coronavirus	Virus resulting in digestive problems.	Virus is spread through infected dog's feces.	Stomach upset evidenced by lack of appetite, vomiting, diarrhea.

inherited diseases are transmitted by both parents, who appear (phenotypically) normal but have a recessive gene for the disease, meaning that they carry, but are not affected by, the disease. These diseases pose serious problems to breeders because in some instances there are no methods of identifying carriers. Often the secondary diseases associated with these skin conditions are even more debilitating than the skin disorders themselves, including cancers and respiratory problems.

Among the hereditary skin disorders, for which the mode of inheritance is known, are acrodermatitis, cutaneous asthenia (Ehlers-Danlos syndrome), sebaceous adenitis, cyclic hematopoiesis, dermatomyositis, IgA deficiency, color dilution alopecia and nodular dermatofibrosis. Some of these disorders are limited to one or two breeds, while others affect a large number of breeds. All inherited diseases must be diagnosed and treated by a veterinary specialist.

PARASITE BITES
Many of us are allergic to insect bites. The bites itch, erupt and may even become infected. Dogs have the same reaction to fleas, ticks and/or mites. When an insect lands on you, you have the chance to whisk it away with your hand.

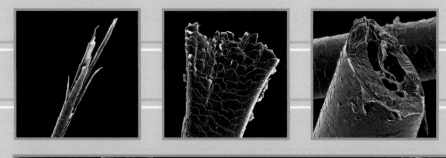

Normal hairs of a dog enlarged 200 times original size. The cuticle (outer covering) is clean and healthy. Unlike human hair that grows from the base, a dog's hair also grows from the end. Damaged hairs and split ends, illustrated above.

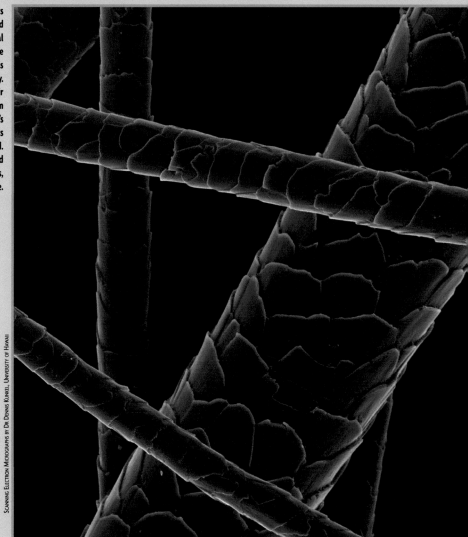

SCANNING ELECTRON MICROGRAPHS BY DR. DENNIS KUNKEL, UNIVERSITY OF HAWAII

Unfortunately, when a dog is bitten by a flea, tick or mite, it can only scratch it away or bite it. By the time the dog has been bitten, the parasite has done some of its damage. It may also have laid eggs, which will cause further problems in the near future. The itching from parasite bites is probably due to the saliva injected into the site when the parasite sucks the dog's blood.

AIRBORNE ALLERGIES
Just as humans suffer from hay fever during the pollinating season, many dogs suffer from the same allergies. When the pollen count is high, your dog might suffer, but don't expect him to sneeze and have a runny nose as a human would. Dogs react to pollen allergies in the same way they react to fleas—they scratch and bite themselves. Dogs, like humans, can be tested for allergens. Discuss the testing with your vet.

ACRAL LICK GRANULOMA
Many breeds have a very poorly understood syndrome called acral lick granuloma. The manifestation of the problem is the dog's tireless attack at a specific area of the body, almost always the legs or paws. The dog licks so intensively that he removes the hair and skin, leaving an ugly, large wound. Tiny protuberances, which are outgrowths of new capillaries,

bead on the surface of the wound. Owners who notice their dogs' biting and chewing at their extremities should have the vet determine the cause. If lick granuloma is identified, although there is no absolute cure, corticosteroids are the most common treatment.

AUTO-IMMUNE ILLNESSES
An auto-immune illness is one in which the immune system overacts and does not recognize parts of the affected person; rather, the immune system starts to react as if these parts were foreign and need to be destroyed. An example is rheumatoid arthritis, which occurs when the body does not recognize the joints, thus leading to a very painful and damaging reaction in the joints. This has nothing to do with age, so can occur in children. The wear-and-tear arthritis of the older person or dog is known as osteoarthritis.

Lupus is an auto-immune disease that affects dogs as well as people. It can take variable forms, affecting the kidneys, bones and the skin. It can be fatal, so is treated with steroids, which can themselves have very significant side effects. The steroids calm down the allergic reaction to the body's tissues, which helps the lupus, but also decreases the body's reaction to real foreign substances such as bacteria, and also thins the skin and bone.

FOOD PROBLEMS

FOOD ALLERGIES

Some dogs can be allergic to many foods that are best-sellers and highly recommended by breeders and vets. Changing the brand of food that you buy may not eliminate the problem if the element to which the dog is allergic is contained in the new brand.

Recognizing a food allergy in a dog can be difficult. Humans often have rashes when they eat foods to which they are allergic, or have swelling of the lips or eyes. Dogs do not usually develop rashes, but react in the same way as they do to an airborne or bite allergy—they itch, scratch and bite. While pollen allergies are usually seasonal, food allergies are year-round problems.

TREATING FOOD ALLERGY

Diagnosis of food allergy is based on a two- to four-week dietary trial with a home-cooked diet fed to the exclusion of all other foods. The diet should consist of boiled rice or potato with a source of protein that the dog has never eaten before, such as fresh or frozen fish, lamb or even something as exotic as pheasant. Water has to be the only drink, and it is really important that no other foods are fed during this trial.

If the dog's condition improves, you will need to try the original diet once again to see if the itching resumes. If it does, then this confirms the diagnosis that the dog is allergic to his original diet. The treatment is long-term feeding of something that does not distress the dog's skin, which may be in the form of one of the commercially available hypoallergenic diets or the home-made diet that you created for the allergy trial.

FOOD INTOLERANCE

Food intolerance is the inability of the dog to completely digest certain foods. This occurs because the dog does not have the chemicals necessary to digest some foodstuffs. These chemicals are called enzymes. All puppies have the enzymes necessary to digest canine milk, but some dogs do not have the enzymes to digest a very different form of milk that is commonly found in human households—milk from cows. In such dogs, drinking cows' milk results in loose bowels, stomach pains and the passage of gas.

Dogs often do not have the enzymes to digest soy or other beans. The treatment is to exclude the foodstuffs that upset your Toller's digestion.

BLOAT/GASTRIC TORSION

Gastric torsion, known commonly as bloat, is a very dangerous problem found in deep-chested breeds. Although it is the subject of much research, bloat still manages to take away many dogs before their time and in a very horrible way.

HOW TO PREVENT BLOAT

Research has confirmed that the structure of deep-chested breeds contributes to their predisposition to bloat. Nevertheless, there are several precautions that you can take to reduce the risk of this condition:

• Feed your dog twice daily rather than offer one big meal.
• Do not exercise your dog for at least one hour before and two hours after he has eaten.
• Make certain that your dog is calm and not overly excited while he is eating. It has been proven that nervous or overly excited dogs are more prone to develop bloat.
• Add a small portion of moist meat product to his dry food ration.
• Serve his meals in an elevated bowl stand, which avoids the dog's craning his neck while eating.
• To prevent your dog from gobbling his food too quickly, and thereby swallowing air, put some large (unswallowable) toys into his bowl so that he will have to eat around them to get his food.
• Do not allow him to gulp water.

DETECTING BLOAT

The following are symptoms of bloat and require immediate veterinary attention:

• Your dog's stomach starts to distend, ending up large and as tight as a football;
• Your dog is dribbling, as no saliva can be swallowed;
• Your dog makes frequent attempts to vomit but cannot bring anything up due to the stomach's being closed off;
• Your dog is distressed from pain;
• Your dog starts to suffer from clinical shock, meaning that there is not enough blood in the dog's circulation as the hard, dilated stomach stops the blood from returning to the heart to be pumped around the body. Clinical shock is indicated by pale gums and tongue, as they have been starved of blood. The shocked dog also has glazed, staring eyes.

You have minutes—yes, *minutes*—to get your dog to the vet. If you see any of these symptoms at any time of the day or night, get to the vet's immediately, as that is where all of the necessary equipment for surgery is located. Someone will have to phone and warn that you are on your way (which is a justification for the invention of the cellular phone!), so that they can be prepared to get your pet on the operating table.

It is possible for a dog to have more than one incident of gastric torsion, even if it has had his stomach stapled, in which the stomach is stapled to the inside of the chest wall to give extra support and prevent its twisting again.

S. E. M. by Dr. Dennis Kunkel, University of Hawaii.

A scanning electron micrograph of a dog flea, *Ctenocephalides canis*, on dog hair.

EXTERNAL PARASITES

FLEAS

Fleas have been around for millions of years and, while we have better tools now for controlling them than at any time in the past, there still is little chance that they will end up on an endangered species list. Actually, they are very well adapted to living on our pets, and they continue to adapt as we make advances.

The female flea can consume 15 times her weight in blood during active reproduction and can lay as many as 40 eggs a day. These eggs are very resistant to the effects of insecticides. They hatch into larvae, which then mature and spin cocoons. The immature fleas reside in this pupal stage until the time is right for feeding. This pupal stage is also very resistant to the effects of insecticides, and pupae can last in the environment without feeding for many months. Newly emergent fleas are attracted to animals by the warmth of the animals' bodies, movement and exhaled carbon dioxide. However, when they first emerge from their cocoons, they orient towards light; thus when an animal passes between a flea and the light source, casting a shadow, the flea pounces and starts to feed. If the animal turns out to be a dog or cat, the reproductive cycle continues. If the flea lands on another type of animal, including a person, the flea will bite but will then look for a more appropriate host. An emerging adult flea can survive without feeding for up to 12 months but, once it tastes blood, it can survive off its host for only 3 to 4 days.

It was once thought that fleas spend most of their lives in the environment, but we now know that fleas won't willingly jump off a dog unless leaping to another dog or when physically removed by brushing, bathing or other manipulation. Flea eggs, on the other hand, are shiny and smooth, and they roll off the animal and into the environment. The eggs, larvae and pupae then exist in the environment, but once the adult finds a susceptible animal, it's home sweet home until the flea is forced to seek refuge elsewhere.

Since adult fleas live on the animal and immature forms survive in the environment, a successful treatment plan must address all stages of the flea life cycle. There are now several safe and effective flea-control products that can be applied on a monthly basis. These

FLEA PREVENTION FOR YOUR DOG
- Discuss with your veterinarian the safest product to protect your dog, likely in the form of a monthly tablet or a liquid preparation placed on the back of the dog's neck.
- For dogs suffering from flea-bite dermatitis, a shampoo or topical insecticide treatment is required.
- Your lawn and property should be sprayed with an insecticide designed to kill fleas and ticks that lurk outdoors.
- Using a flea comb, check the dog's coat regularly for any signs of parasites.
- Practice good housekeeping. Vacuum floors, carpets and furniture regularly, especially in the areas that the dog frequents, and wash the dog's bedding weekly.
- Follow up house-cleaning with carpet shampoos and sprays to rid the house of fleas at all stages of development. Insect growth regulators are the safest option.

include fipronil, imidacloprid, selamectin and permethrin (found in several formulations). Most of these products have significant flea-killing rates within 24 hours. However, none of them will control the immature forms in the environment. To accomplish this, there are a variety of insect growth regulators that can be sprayed into the

THE FLEA'S LIFE CYCLE

What came first, the flea or the egg? This age-old mystery is more difficult to comprehend than the actual cycle of the flea. Fleas usually live only about four months. A female can lay 2,000 eggs in her lifetime.

Egg

After ten days of rolling around your carpet or under your furniture, the eggs hatch into larvae, which feed on various and sundry debris. In days or months, depending on the climate, the larvae spin cocoons and develop into the pupal or nymph stage, which quickly develop into fleas.

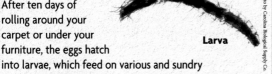

Larva

Photo by Carolina Biological Supply Co.

Pupa

These immature fleas must locate a host within 10 to 14 days or they will die. Only about 1% of the flea population exist as adult fleas, while the other 99% exist as eggs, larvae or pupae.

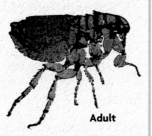

Adult

KILL FLEAS THE NATURAL WAY

If you choose not to go the route of conventional medication, there are some natural ways to ward off fleas:

- Dust your dog with a natural flea powder, composed of such herbal goodies as rosemary, wormwood, pennyroyal, citronella, rue, tobacco powder and eucalyptus.
- Apply diatomaceous earth, the fossilized remains of single-cell algae, to your carpets, furniture and pet's bedding. Even though it's not good for dogs, it's even worse for fleas, which will dry up swiftly and die.
- Brush your dog frequently, give him adequate exercise and let him fast occasionally. All of these activities strengthen the dog's immune system and make him more resistant to disease and parasites.
- Bathe your dog with a capful of pennyroyal or eucalyptus oil.
- Feed a natural diet, free of additives and preservatives. Add some fresh garlic and brewer's yeast to the dog's morning portion, as these items have flea-repelling properties.

environment (e.g., pyriproxyfen, methoprene, fenoxycarb) as well as insect development inhibitors such as lufenuron that can be administered. These compounds have no effect on adult fleas, but they stop immature forms from developing into adults.

In years gone by, we relied heavily on toxic insecticides (such as organophosphates, organochlorines and carbamates) to manage the flea problem, but today's options are not only much safer to use on our pets but also safer for the environment.

TICKS

Ticks are members of the spider class (arachnids) and are blood-sucking parasites capable of transmitting a variety of diseases, including Lyme disease, ehrlichiosis, babesiosis and Rocky Mountain spotted fever. It's easy to see ticks on your own skin, but it is more of a challenge when your furry companion is affected. Whenever you happen to be planning a stroll in a tick-infested area (especially forests, grassy or wooded areas or parks) be prepared to do a thorough inspection of your dog afterward to search for ticks. Ticks can be tricky, so make sure you spend time looking in the ears, between the toes and everywhere else where a tick might hide. Ticks need to be attached for 24–72 hours before they transmit most of the diseases that they carry, so you do have a window of opportunity for some preventive intervention.

S. E. M. by Phototake.

A scanning electron micrograph of the head of a female deer tick, *Ixodes dammini*, a parasitic tick that carries Lyme disease.

A TICKING BOMB

There is nothing good about a tick's harpooning his nose into your dog's skin. Among the diseases caused by ticks are Rocky Mountain spotted fever, canine ehrlichiosis, canine babesiosis, canine hepatozoonosis and Lyme disease. If a dog is allergic to the saliva of a female wood tick, he can develop tick paralysis.

Female ticks live to eat and breed. They can lay between 4,000 and 5,000 eggs and they die soon after. Males, on the other hand, live only to mate with the females and continue the process as long as they are able. Most ticks live on multiple hosts before parasitizing dogs. The immature forms typically reside on grass and shrubs, waiting for susceptible animals to walk by. The larvae and nymph stages typically feed on wildlife.

If only a few ticks are present on a dog, they can be plucked out, but it is important to remove the entire head and

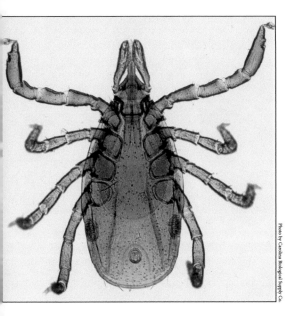

Photo by Carolina Biological Supply Co.

Deer tick,
Ixodes dammini.

be disposed of in a container of alcohol or household bleach.

Some of the newer flea products, specifically those with fipronil, selamectin and permethrin, have effect against some, but not all, species of tick. Flea collars containing appropriate pesticides (e.g., propoxur, chlorfenvinphos) can aid in tick control. In most areas, such collars should be placed on animals in March, at the beginning of the tick season, and changed regularly. Leaving the collar on when the pesticide level is waning invites the development of resistance. Amitraz collars are also good for tick control, and the active ingredient does not interfere with other flea-control products. The ingredient helps prevent the attachment of ticks to the skin and will cause those ticks already on the skin to detach themselves.

mouthparts, which may be deeply embedded in the skin. This is best accomplished with forceps designed especially for this purpose; fingers can be used but should be protected with rubber gloves, plastic wrap or at least a paper towel. The tick should be grasped as closely as possible to the animal's skin and should be pulled upward with steady, even pressure. Do not squeeze, crush or puncture the body of the tick or you risk exposure to any disease carried by that tick. Once the ticks have been removed, the sites of attachment should be disinfected. Your hands should then be washed with soap and water to further minimize risk of contagion. The tick should

TICK CONTROL

Removal of underbrush and leaf litter and the thinning of trees in areas where tick control is desired are recommended. These actions remove the cover and food sources for small animals that serve as hosts for ticks. With continued mowing of grasses in these areas, the probability of ticks' surviving is further reduced. A variety of insecticide ingredients (e.g., resmethrin, carbaryl, permethrin, chlorpyrifos, dioxathion and allethrin) are registered for tick control around the home.

MITES

Mites are tiny arachnid parasites that parasitize the skin of dogs. Skin diseases caused by mites are referred to as "mange," and there are many different forms seen in dogs. These forms are very different from one another, each one warranting an individual description.

Sarcoptic mange, or scabies, is one of the itchiest conditions that affects dogs. The microscopic *Sarcoptes* mites burrow into the superficial layers of the skin and can drive dogs crazy with itchiness. They are also communicable to people, although they can't complete their reproductive cycle on people. In addition to being tiny, the mites also are often difficult to find when trying to make a diagnosis. Skin scrapings from multiple areas are examined microscopically but, even then, sometimes the mites cannot be found.

Fortunately, scabies is relatively easy to treat, and there are a variety of products that will successfully kill the mites. Since the mites can't live in the environment for very long without feeding, a complete cure is usually possible within four to eight weeks.

Cheyletiellosis is caused by a relatively large mite, which sometimes can be seen even without a microscope. Often referred to as "walking dandruff," this also causes itching, but not usually as profound as with scabies. While *Cheyletiella* mites can survive somewhat longer in

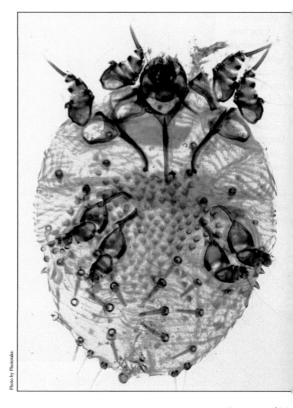

Photo by Phototake.

Sarcoptes scabiei, commonly known as the "itch mite."

the environment than scabies mites, they too are relatively easy to treat, being responsive to not only the medications used to treat scabies but also often to flea-control products.

Otodectes cynotis is the canine ear mite and is one of the more common causes of mange, especially in young dogs in shelters or pet stores. That's because the mites are typically present in large numbers and are quickly spread to nearby animals. The mites rarely do

Micrograph of a dog louse, *Heterodoxus spiniger*. Female lice attach their eggs to the hairs of the dog. As the eggs hatch, the larval lice bite and feed on the blood. Lice can also feed on dead skin and hair. This feeding activity can cause hair loss and skin problems.

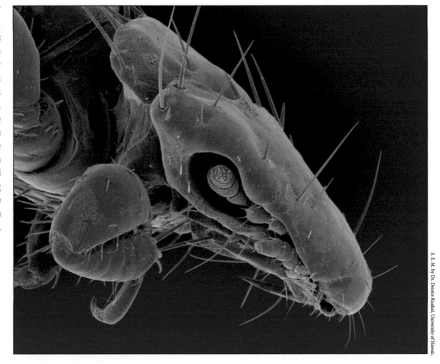

S. E. M. by Dr. Dennis Kunkel, University of Hawaii.

much harm but can be difficult to eradicate if the treatment regimen is not comprehensive. While many try to treat the condition with ear drops only, this is the most common cause of treatment failure. Ear drops cause the mites to simply move out of the ears and as far away as possible (usually to the base of the tail) until the insecticide levels in the ears drop to an acceptable level—then it's back to business as usual! The successful treatment of ear mites requires treating all animals in the household with a systemic insecticide, such as selamectin, or a combination of miticidal ear

drops combined with whole-body flea-control preparations.

Demodicosis, sometimes referred to as red mange, can be one of the most difficult forms of mange to treat. Part of the problem has to do with the fact that the mites live in the hair follicles and they are relatively well shielded from topical and systemic products. The main issue, however, is that demodectic mange typically results only when there is some underlying process interfering with the dog's immune system.

Since Demodex mites are normal residents of the skin of

mammals, including humans, there is usually a mite population explosion only when the immune system fails to keep the number of mites in check. In young animals, the immune deficit may be transient or may reflect an actual inherited immune problem. In older animals, demodicosis is usually seen only when there is another disease hampering the immune system, such as diabetes, cancer, thyroid problems or the use of immune-suppressing drugs. Accordingly, treatment involves not only trying to kill the mange mites but also discerning what is interfering with immune function and correcting it if possible.

Chiggers represent several different species of mite that don't parasitize dogs specifically, but do latch on to passersby and can cause irritation. The problem is most prevalent in wooded areas in the late summer and fall. Treatment is not difficult, as the mites do not complete their life cycle on dogs and are susceptible to a variety of miticidal products.

Mosquitoes

Mosquitoes have long been known to transmit a variety of diseases to people, as well as just being biting pests during warm weather. They also pose a real risk to pets. Not only

Illustration by Photozide.

Illustration of **Demodex folliculoram.**

do they carry deadly heartworms but recently there also has been much concern over their involvement with West Nile virus. While we can avoid heartworm with the use of preventive medications, there are no such preventives for West Nile virus. The only method of prevention in endemic areas is active mosquito control. Fortunately, most dogs that have been exposed to the virus only developed flu-like symptoms and, to date, there have not been the large number of reported deaths in canines as seen in some other species.

MOSQUITO REPELLENT

Low concentrations of DEET (less than 10%), found in many human mosquito repellents, have been safely used on dogs but, in these concentrations, probably give only about two hours of protection. DEET may be safe in these small concentrations, but since it is not licensed for use on dogs, there is no research proving its safety for dogs. Products containing permethrin give the longest-lasting protection, perhaps two to four weeks. As DEET is not licensed for use on dogs, and both DEET and permethrin can be quite toxic to cats, appropriate care should be exercised. Other products, such as those containing oil of citronella, also have some mosquito-repellent activity, but typically have a relatively short duration of action.

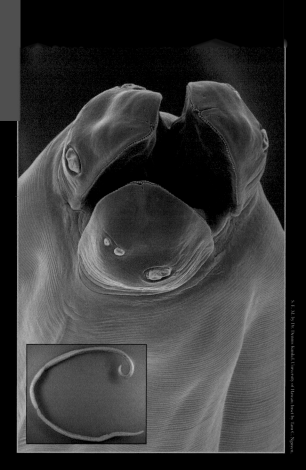

The ascarid roundworm *Toxocara canis*, showing the mouth with three lips. Inset: photomicrograph of the roundworm *Ascaris lumbricoides*.

S.E.M. by Dr. Dennis Kunkel, University of Hawaii. Inset by Tami C. Nguyen.

ASCARID DANGERS

The most commonly encountered worms in dogs are roundworms known as ascarids. *Toxascaris leonine* and Toxocara canis are the two species that infect dogs. Subsisting in the dog's stomach and intestines, adult roundworms can grow to 7 inches in length and adult females can lay in excess of 200,000 eggs in a single day.

In humans, visceral larval migrans affects people who have ingested eggs of Toxocara canis, which frequently contaminates children's sandboxes, beaches and park grounds. The roundworms reside in the human's stomach and intestines, as they would in a dog's, but do not mature. Instead, they find their way to the liver, lungs and skin, or even to the heart or kidneys in severe cases. Deworming puppies is critical in preventing the infection in humans, and young children should never handle nursing pups who have not been dewormed.

INTERNAL PARASITES: WORMS

ASCARIDS

Ascarids are intestinal roundworms that rarely cause severe disease in dogs. Nonetheless, they are of major public health significance because they can be transferred to people. Sadly, it is children who are most commonly affected by the parasite, probably from inadvertently ingesting ascarid-contaminated soil. In fact, many yards and children's sandboxes contain appreciable numbers of ascarid eggs. So, while ascarids don't bite dogs or latch onto their intestines to suck blood, they do cause some nasty medical conditions in children and are best eradicated from our furry friends. Because pups can start passing ascarid eggs by three weeks of age, most parasite-control programs begin at two weeks of age and are repeated every two weeks until pups are eight weeks old. It is important

HOOKED ON ANCYLOSTOMA

Adult dogs can become infected by the bloodsucking nematodes we commonly call hookworms via ingesting larvae from the ground or via the larvae penetrating the dog's skin. It is not uncommon for infected dogs to show no symptoms of hookworm infestation. Sometimes symptoms occur within ten days of exposure. These symptoms can include bloody diarrhea, anemia, loss of weight and general weakness. Dogs pass the hookworm eggs in their stools, which serves as the vet's method of identifying the infestation. The hookworm larvae can encyst themselves in the dog's tissues and be released when the dog is experiencing stress.

Caused by an Ancylostoma species whose common host is the dog, cutaneous larval migrans affects humans, causing itching and lumps and streaks beneath the surface of the skin.

S. E. M. by Dr. Dennis Kunkel, University of Hawaii

to realize that bitches can pass ascarids to their pups even if they test negative prior to whelping. Accordingly, bitches are best treated at the same time as the pups.

HOOKWORMS

Unlike ascarids, hookworms do latch onto a dog's intestinal tract and can cause significant loss of blood and protein. Similar to ascarids, hookworms can be transmitted to humans, where they cause a condition known as cutaneous larval migrans. Dogs can become infected either by consuming the infective larvae or by the larvae's penetrating the skin directly. People most often get infected when they are lying on the ground (such as on a beach) and the larvae penetrate the skin. Yes, the larvae can penetrate through a beach blanket. Hookworms are typically susceptible to the same medications used to treat ascarids.

The hookworm *Ancylostoma caninum* infests the intestines of dogs.

Inset: Note the row of hooks at the posterior end used to anchor the worm to the intestinal wall.

WHIPWORMS

Whipworms latch onto the lower aspects of the dog's colon and can cause cramping and diarrhea. Eggs do not start to appear in the dog's feces until about three months after the dog was infected. This worm has a peculiar life cycle, which makes it more difficult to control than ascarids or hookworms. The good thing is that whipworms rarely are transferred to people.

Some of the medications used to treat ascarids and hookworms are also effective against whipworms, but, in general, a separate treatment protocol is needed. Since most of the medications are effective against the adults but not the eggs or larvae, treatment is typically repeated in three weeks, and then

Adult whipworm, *Trichuris* sp., an intestinal parasite.

S. E. M. by Dr. Dennis Kunkel, University of Hawaii.

WORM-CONTROL GUIDELINES

- Practice sanitary habits with your dog and home.
- Clean up after your dog and don't let him sniff or eat other dogs' droppings.
- Control insects and fleas in the dog's environment. Fleas, lice, cockroaches, beetles, mice and rats can act as hosts for various worms.
- Prevent dogs from eating uncooked meat, raw poultry and dead animals.
- Keep dogs and children from playing in sand and soil.
- Kennel dogs on cement or gravel; avoid dirt runs.
- Administer heartworm preventives regularly.
- Have your vet examine your dog's stools at your annual visits.
- Select a boarding kennel carefully so as to avoid contamination from other dogs or an unsanitary environment.
- Prevent dogs from roaming. Obey local leash laws.

often in three months as well. Unfortunately, since dogs don't develop resistance to whipworms, it is difficult to prevent them from getting reinfected if they visit soil contaminated with whipworm eggs.

TAPEWORMS

There are many different species of tapeworm that affect dogs, but *Dipylidium caninum* is probably the most common and is spread by fleas. Flea larvae feed on organic debris and tapeworm eggs in the environment and, when a dog chews at himself and manages to ingest fleas, he might get a dose of tapeworm at the same time. The tapeworm then develops further in the intestine of the dog.

The tapeworm itself, which is a parasitic flatworm that latches onto the intestinal wall, is composed of numerous segments. When the segments break off into the intestine (as proglottids), they may accumulate around the rectum like grains of rice. While this tapeworm is disgusting in its behavior, it is not directly communicable to humans (although humans can also get infected by swallowing fleas).

A much more dangerous flatworm is Echinococcus multilocularis, which is typically found in foxes, coyotes and wolves. The eggs are passed in the feces and infect rodents, and, when dogs eat the rodents, the dogs can be infected by thousands of adult tapeworms. While the parasites don't cause many problems in dogs, this is considered the most lethal worm infection that people can get. Take appropriate precautions if you live in an area in which these tapeworms are found. Do not use mulch that may contain feces of dogs, cats or wildlife, and discourage your pets from hunting wildlife. Treat these tapeworm infections aggressively in pets, because if humans get infected, approximately half die.

HEARTWORMS

Heartworm disease is caused by the parasite Dirofilaria immitis and is seen in dogs around the world. A member of the roundworm group, it is spread between dogs by the bite of an infected mosquito. The mosquito injects infective larvae into the dog's skin with its bite, and these larvae develop under the skin for a period of time before making their way to the heart. There they develop into adults, which grow and create blockages of the heart, lungs and major blood vessels there. They also start producing offspring (microfilariae), and

A dog tapeworm proglottid (body segment).

The dog tapeworm *Taenia pisiformis.*

S. E. M. by Dr. Dennis Kunkel, University of Hawaii.

A Look at Internal Parasites

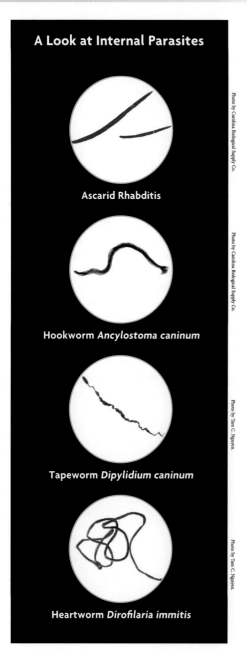

Ascarid Rhabditis

Hookworm *Ancylostoma caninum*

Tapeworm *Dipylidium caninum*

Heartworm *Dirofilaria immitis*

Photo by Carolina Biological Supply Co.

Photo by Carolina Biological Supply Co.

Photo by Tam C. Nguyen.

Photo by Tam C. Nguyen.

these microfilariae circulate in the bloodstream, waiting to hitch a ride when the next mosquito bites. Once in the mosquito, the microfilariae develop into infective larvae and the entire process is repeated.

When dogs get infected with heartworm, over time they tend to develop symptoms associated with heart disease, such as coughing, exercise intolerance and potentially many other manifestations. Diagnosis is confirmed by either seeing the microfilariae themselves in blood samples or using immunologic tests (antigen testing) to identify the presence of adult heartworms. Since antigen tests measure the presence of adult heartworms and microfilarial tests measure offspring produced by adults, neither are positive until six to seven months after the initial infection. However, the beginning of damage can occur by fifth-stage larvae as early as three months after infection. Thus it is possible for dogs to be harboring problem-causing larvae for up to three months before either type of test would identify an infection.

The good news is that there are great protocols available for preventing heartworm in dogs. Testing is critical in the process, and it is important to understand the benefits as well as the limitations of such testing. All dogs six months of age or older that have not been on continuous heartworm-preventive medication should

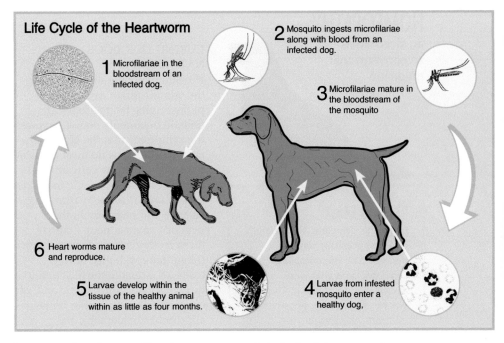

Life Cycle of the Heartworm

1 Microfilariae in the bloodstream of an infected dog.

2 Mosquito ingests microfilariae along with blood from an infected dog.

3 Microfilariae mature in the bloodstream of the mosquito

4 Larvae from infested mosquito enter a healthy dog,

5 Larvae develop within the tissue of the healthy animal within as little as four months.

6 Heart worms mature and reproduce.

be screened with microfilarial or antigen tests. For dogs receiving preventive medication, periodic antigen testing helps assess the effectiveness of the preventives. The American Heartworm Society guidelines suggest that annual retesting may not be necessary when owners have absolutely provided continuous heartworm prevention. Retesting on a two- to three-year interval may be sufficient in these cases. However, your veterinarian will likely have specific guidelines under which heartworm preventives will be prescribed, and many prefer to err on the side of safety and retest annually.

It is indeed fortunate that heartworm is relatively easy to prevent, because treatments can be as life-threatening as the disease itself. Treatment requires a two-step process that kills the adult heartworms first and then the microfilariae. Prevention is obviously preferable; this involves a once-monthly oral or topical treatment. The most common oral preventives include ivermectin (not suitable for some breeds), moxidectin and milbemycin oxime; the once-a-month topical drug selamectin provides heartworm protection in addition to flea, some types of tick and other parasite controls.

HOMEOPATHY:
an alternative to conventional medicine

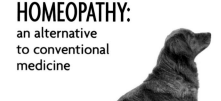

"Less is Most"

Using this principle, the strength of a homeopathic remedy is measured by the number of serial dilutions that were undertaken to create it. The greater the number of serial dilutions, the greater the strength of the homeopathic remedy. The potency of a remedy that has been made by making a dilution of 1 part in 100 parts (or 1/100) is 1c or 1cH. If this remedy is subjected to a series of further dilutions, each one being 1/100, a more dilute and stronger remedy is produced. If the remedy is diluted in this way six times, it is called 6c or 6cH. A dilution of 6c is 1 part in 1,000,000,000,000. In general, higher potencies in more frequent doses are better for acute symptoms and lower potencies in more infrequent doses are more useful for chronic, long-standing problems.

CURING OUR DOGS NATURALLY

Holistic medicine means treating the whole animal as a unique, perfect living being. Generally, holistic treatments do not suppress the symptoms that the body naturally produces, as do most medications prescribed by conventional doctors and vets. Holistic methods seek to cure disease by regaining balance and harmony in the patient's environment. Some of these methods include use of nutritional therapy, herbs, flower essences, aromatherapy, acupuncture, massage, chiropractic and, of course, the most popular holistic approach, homeopathy.

Homeopathy is a theory or system of treating illness with small doses of substances which, if administered in larger quantities, would produce the symptoms that the patient already has. This approach is often described as "like cures like." Although modern veterinary medicine is geared toward the "quick fix," homeopathy relies on the belief that, given the time, the body is able to heal itself and return to its natural, healthy state.

Choosing a remedy to cure a problem in our dogs is the difficult part of homeopathy. Consult with your vet for a professional diagnosis of your dog's symptoms. Often these symptoms require immediate conventional care. If your vet is willing and knowledgeable, you may attempt a homeopathic remedy. Be aware that cortisone prevents homeopathic remedies from working. There are hundreds of possibilities and combinations to cure many problems in dogs, from basic physical problems such as excessive shedding, fleas or other parasites, unattractive doggy odor, bad breath, upset tummy, obesity, dry, oily or dull coat, diarrhea, ear problems or eye discharge (including tears and dry or mucousy matter), to behavioral abnormalities such as fear of loud noises, habitual licking, poor appetite, excessive barking and various phobias. From alumina to zincum metallicum, the remedies span the planet and the imagination...from flowers and weeds to chemicals, insect droppings, diesel smoke and volcanic ash.

Using "Like to Treat Like"

Unlike conventional medicines that suppress symptoms, homeopathic remedies treat illnesses with small doses of substances that, if administered in larger quantities, would produce the symptoms that the patient already has. While the same homeopathic remedy can be used to treat different symptoms in different dogs, here are some interesting remedies and their uses.

Apis Mellifica
(made from honey bee venom) can be used for allergies or to reduce swelling that occurs in acutely infected kidneys.

Diesel Smoke
can be used to help control travel sickness.

Calcarea Fluorica
(made from calcium fluoride, which helps harden bone structure) can be useful in treating hard lumps in tissues.

Natrum Muriaticum
(made from common salt, sodium chloride) is useful in treating thin, thirsty dogs.

Nitricum Acidum
(made from nitric acid) is used for symptoms you would expect to see from contact with acids, such as lesions, especially where the skin joins the linings of body orifices or openings such as the lips and nostrils.

Symphytum
(made from the herb Knitbone, *Symphytum officianale*) is used to encourage bones to heal.

Urtica Urens
(made from the common stinging nettle) is used in treating painful, irritating rashes.

HOMEOPATHIC REMEDIES FOR YOUR DOG

Symptom/Ailment	Possible Remedy
ALLERGIES	Apis Mellifica 30c, Astacus Fluviatilis 6c, Pulsatilla 30c, Urtica Urens 6c
ALOPECIA	Alumina 30c, Lycopodium 30c, Sepia 30c, Thallium 6c
ANAL GLANDS (BLOCKED)	Hepar Sulphuris Calcareum 30c, Sanicula 6c, Silicea 6c
ARTHRITIS	Rhus Toxicodendron 6c, Bryonia Alba 6c
CATARACT	Calcarea Carbonica 6c, Conium Maculatum 6c, Phosphorus 30c, Silicea 30c
CONSTIPATION	Alumina 6c, Carbo Vegetabilis 30c, Graphites 6c, Nitricum Acidum 30c, Silicea 6c
COUGHING	Aconitum Napellus 6c, Belladonna 30c, Hyoscyamus Niger 30c, Phosphorus 30c
DIARRHEA	Arsenicum Album 30c, Aconitum Napellus 6c, Chamomilla 30c, Mercurius Corrosivus 30c
DRY EYE	Zincum Metallicum 30c
EAR PROBLEMS	Aconitum Napellus 30c, Belladonna 30c, Hepar Sulphuris 30c, Tellurium 30c, Psorinum 200c
EYE PROBLEMS	Borax 6c, Aconitum Napellus 30c, Graphites 6c, Staphysagria 6c, Thuja Occidentalis 30c
GLAUCOMA	Aconitum Napellus 30c, Apis Mellifica 6c, Phosphorus 30c
HEAT STROKE	Belladonna 30c, Gelsemium Sempervirens 30c, Sulphur 30c
HICCOUGHS	Cinchona Deficinalis 6c
HIP DYSPLASIA	Colocynthis 6c, Rhus Toxicodendron 6c, Bryonia Alba 6c
INCONTINENCE	Argentum Nitricum 6c, Causticum 30c, Conium Maculatum 30c, Pulsatilla 30c, Sepia 30c
INSECT BITES	Apis Mellifica 30c, Cantharis 30c, Hypericum Perforatum 6c, Urtica Urens 30c
ITCHING	Alumina 30c, Arsenicum Album 30c, Carbo Vegetabilis 30c, Hypericum Perforatum 6c, Mezerium 6c, Sulphur 30c
KENNEL COUGH	Drosera 6c, Ipecacuanha 30c
MASTITIS	Apis Mellifica 30c, Belladonna 30c, Urtica Urens 1m
MOTION SICKNESS	Cocculus 6c, Petroleum 6c
PATELLAR LUXATION	Gelsemium Sempervirens 6c, Rhus Toxicodendron 6c
PENIS PROBLEMS	Aconitum Napellus 30c, Hepar Sulphuris Calcareum 30c, Pulsatilla 30c, Thuja Occidentalis 6c
PUPPY TEETHING	Calcarea Carbonica 6c, Chamomilla 6c, Phytolacca 6c

Recognizing a Sick Dog

Unlike colicky babies and cranky children, our canine charges cannot tell us when they are feeling ill. Therefore, there are a number of signs that owners can identify to know that their dogs are not feeling well.

**Take note for
physical manifestations such as:**

- unusual, bad odor, including bad breath
- excessive shedding
- wax in the ears, chronic ear irritation
- oily, flaky, dull haircoat
- mucus, tearing or similar discharge in the eyes
- fleas or mites
- mucus in stool, diarrhea
- sensitivity to petting or handling
- licking at paws, scratching face, etc.

**Keep an eye out for
behavioral changes as well including:**

- lethargy, idleness
- lack of patience or general irritability
- lack of appetite
- phobias (fear of people, loud noises, etc.)
- strange behavior, suspicion, fear
- coprophagia
- more frequent barking
- whimpering, crying

Get Well Soon

You don't need a DVM to provide good TLC to your sick or recovering dog, but you do need to pay attention to some details that normally wouldn't bother him. The following tips will aid Fido's recovery and get him back on his paws again:

- Keep his space free of irritating smells, like heavy perfumes and air fresheners.
- Rest is the best medicine! Avoid harsh lighting that will prevent your dog from sleeping. Shade him from bright sunlight during the day and dim the lights in the evening.
- Keep the noise level down. Animals are more sensitive to sound when they are sick.

- Be attentive to any necessary temperature adjustments. A dog with a fever needs a cool room and cold liquids. A bitch that is whelping or recovering from surgery will be more comfortable in a warm room, consuming warm liquids and food.
- You wouldn't send a sick child back to school early, so don't rush your dog back into a full routine until he seems absolutely ready.

Number-One Killer Disease in Dogs: CANCER

In every age, there is a word associated with a disease or plague that causes humans to shudder. In the 21st century, that word is "cancer." Just as cancer is the leading cause of death in humans, it claims nearly half the lives of dogs that die from a natural disease as well as half the dogs that die over the age of ten years.

Described as a genetic disease, cancer becomes a greater risk as the dog ages. Vets and dog owners have become increasingly aware of the threat of cancer to dogs. Statistics reveal that one dog in every five will develop cancer, the most common of which is skin cancer. Many cancers, including prostate, ovarian and breast cancer, can be avoided by spaying and neutering our dogs by the age of six months.

Early detection of cancer can save or extend a dog's life, so it is absolutely vital for owners to have their dogs examined by a qualified vet or oncologist immediately upon detection of any abnormality. Certain dietary guidelines have also proven to reduce the onset and spread of cancer. Foods based on fish rather than beef, due to the presence of Omega-3 fatty acids, are recommended. Other amino acids such as glutamine have significant benefits for canines, particularly those breeds that show a greater susceptibility to cancer.

Cancer management and treatments promise hope for future generations of canines. Since the disease is genetic, breeders should never breed a dog whose parents, grandparents and any related siblings have developed cancer. It is difficult to know whether to exclude an otherwise healthy dog from a breeding program as the disease does not manifest itself until the dog's senior years.

RECOGNIZE CANCER WARNING SIGNS

Since early detection can possibly rescue your dog from becoming a cancer statistic, it is essential for owners to recognize the possible signs and seek the assistance of a qualified professional.

- Abnormal bumps or lumps that continue to grow
- Bleeding or discharge from any body cavity
- Persistent stiffness or lameness
- Recurrent sores or sores that do not heal
- Inappetence
- Breathing difficulties
- Weight loss
- Bad breath or odors
- General malaise and fatigue
- Eating and swallowing problems
- Difficulty urinating and defecating

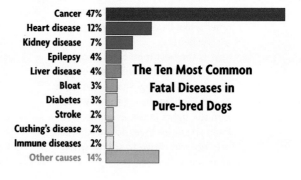

Cancer	47%
Heart disease	12%
Kidney disease	7%
Epilepsy	4%
Liver disease	4%
Bloat	3%
Diabetes	3%
Stroke	2%
Cushing's disease	2%
Immune diseases	2%
Other causes	14%

The Ten Most Common Fatal Diseases in Pure-bred Dogs

CDS: COGNITIVE DYSFUNCTION SYNDROME
"OLD-DOG SYNDROME"

There are many ways to evaluate old-dog syndrome. Vets have defined CDS (cognitive dysfunction syndrome) as the gradual deterioration of cognitive abilities. These are indicated by changes in the dog's behavior. When a dog changes his routine response, and maladies have been eliminated as the cause of these behavioral changes, then CDS is the usual diagnosis.

More than half the dogs over eight years old suffer some form of CDS. The older the dog, the more chance it has of suffering from CDS. In humans, doctors often dismiss the CDS behavioral changes as part of "winding down."

There are four major signs of CDS: frequent potty accidents inside the home, sleeping much more or much less than normal, acting confused and failing to respond to social stimuli.

SYMPTOMS OF CDS

FREQUENT POTTY ACCIDENTS
- *Urinates in the house.*
- *Defecates in the house.*
- *Doesn't signal that he wants to go out.*

SLEEP PATTERNS
- *Moves much more slowly.*
- *Sleeps more than normal during the day.*
- *Sleeps less during the night.*

CONFUSION
- *Goes outside and just stands there.*
- *Appears confused with a faraway look in his eyes.*
- *Hides more often.*
- *Doesn't recognize friends.*
- *Doesn't come when called.*
- *Walks around listlessly and without a destination.*

FAILURE TO RESPOND TO SOCIAL STIMULI
- *Comes to people less frequently, whether called or not.*
- *Doesn't tolerate petting for more than a short time.*
- *Doesn't come to the door when you return home.*

NOVA SCOTIA DUCK TOLLING RETRIEVER

The term *old* is a qualitative term. For dogs, as well as for their masters, *old* is relative. Certainly we can all distinguish between a puppy Toller and an adult Toller—there are the obvious physical traits, such as size, appearance and facial expressions, as well as personality traits. Puppies and young dogs like to play with children. Children's natural exuberance is a good match for the seemingly endless energy of young dogs. They like to run, jump, chase and retrieve. When dogs grow older and cease their interaction with children, they are often thought of as being too old to keep pace with the children. On the other hand, if a Toller is only exposed to people with quieter lifestyles, his life will normally be less active and the decrease in his activity level as he ages will not be as obvious.

If people live to be 100 years old, dogs live to be 20 years old. While this might seem like a good rule of thumb, it is very inaccurate. When trying to compare dog years to human years, you cannot make a generalization about all dogs. Toller owners are lucky in that they have a long-lived breed, with the average lifespan being 12 to 16 years.

Dogs in general are considered physically mature at three years of age (or earlier), but can reproduce even earlier. So, again to generalize, the first three years of a dog's life are like seven times that of comparable humans. That means a 3-year-old dog is like a 21-year-old human. However, as the curve of comparison shows, there is no hard and fast rule for comparing dog and human ages. Small breeds tend to live longer than large breeds, some breeds' adolescent periods last longer than

GETTING OLD

The bottom line is simply that your dog is getting old when you think he is getting old because he slows down in his level of general activity, including walking, running, eating, jumping and retrieving. On the other hand, the frequency of certain activities increases, such as more sleeping, more barking and more repetition of habits like going to the door without being called when you put your coat on to leave the house.

others' and some breeds experience rapid periods of growth. The comparison is made even more difficult, for, likewise, not all humans age at the same rate...and human females live longer than human males.

WHAT TO LOOK FOR IN SENIORS

Most vets and behaviorists use the seven-year mark as the time to consider a dog a *senior*. This term does not imply that the dog is geriatric and has begun to fail in mind and body. Aging is essentially a slowing process. Humans readily admit that they feel a difference in their activity level from age 20 to 30, and then from 30 to 40, etc. By treating the

seven-year-old dog as a senior, owners are able to implement certain therapeutic and preventative medical strategies with the help of their vets.

A special-care program should include at least two veterinary visits per year and screening sessions to determine the dog's health status, as well as nutritional counseling. Vets determine a senior dog's health status through a blood smear for a complete blood count, serum chemistry profile with electrolytes, urinalysis, blood pressure check, electrocardiogram, ocular tonometry (pressure on the eyeball) and dental prophylaxis.

Such an extensive program for senior dogs is well advised before

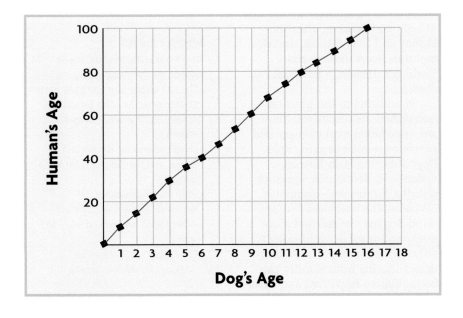

Nova Scotia Duck Tollers of various ages. The Toller is an active dog that retains much of his energy into his "double digits." It's hard to tell which of these dogs are older just by looking!

owners start to see the obvious physical signs of aging, such as slower and inhibited movement, graying, increased sleep/nap periods and disinterest in play and other activity. This preventative program promises a longer, healthier life for the aging dog. Among the physical problems common in aging dogs are the loss of sight and hearing, arthritis, kidney and liver failure, diabetes mellitus, heart disease and Cushing's disease (a hormonal disease).

In addition to the physical manifestations discussed, there are some behavioral changes and problems related to aging dogs. Dogs suffering from hearing or vision loss, dental discomfort or arthritis can become aggressive. Likewise, the near-deaf and/or blind dog may be startled more easily and react in an unexpectedly aggressive manner. Senior dogs suffering from senility can become more impatient and irrita-

ble. Potty accidents are associated with loss of mobility, kidney problems and loss of sphincter control as well as plaque accumulation, physiological brain changes and reactions to medications. Older dogs, just like young puppies, suffer from separation anxiety, which can lead to exces-

SENIOR SIGNS

An old dog starts to show one or more of the following symptoms:

- The hair on the face and paws starts to turn gray. The color breakdown usually starts around the eyes and mouth.
- Sleep patterns are deeper and longer, and the old dog is harder to awaken.
- Food intake diminishes.
- Responses to calls, whistles and other signals are ignored more and more.
- Eye contact does not evoke tail wagging (assuming it once did).

sive barking, whining, housesoiling and destructive behavior. Aging dogs may become fearful of everyday sounds, such as vacuum cleaners, heaters, thunder and passing traffic. Some may have difficulty sleeping, due to discomfort, the need for frequent toilet visits and the like.

Owners should avoid spoiling the older dog with too many fatty treats. Obesity is a common problem in older dogs and subtracts years from their lives. Keep the senior dog as trim as possible, since excessive weight puts additional stress on the body's vital organs. Some breeders recommend supplementing the diet with foods high in fiber and lower in calories. Adding fresh vegetables and marrow broth to the senior's diet makes a tasty, low-calorie, low-fat supplement. Vets also offer specialty diets for senior dogs that are worth exploring.

Your dog, as he nears his twilight years, needs your patience and good care more than ever. Never punish an older dog for an accident or abnormal behavior. For all the years of love, protection and companionship that your dog has provided, he deserves special attention and courtesies. The older dog may need to relieve himself at 3 a.m. because he can no longer hold it for eight hours. Older dogs may not be able to remain crated for more than two or three hours. It may be time to give up a sofa or chair to your old friend. Although he may not seem as enthusiastic about your attention and petting, he does appreciate the considerations you offer as he gets older.

Your Toller does not understand why his world is slowing

NOTICING THE SYMPTOMS

The symptoms listed below are symptoms that gradually appear and become more noticeable. They are not life-threatening; however, the symptoms below are to be taken very seriously and warrant a discussion with your vet:

- Your dog cries and whimpers when he moves, and he stops running completely.
- Convulsions start or become more serious and frequent. The usual convulsion (spasm) is when the dog stiffens and starts to tremble, being unable or unwilling to move. The seizure usually lasts for 5 to 30 minutes.
- Your dog drinks more water and urinates more frequently. Wetting and bowel accidents take place indoors without warning.
- Vomiting becomes more and more frequent.

down. Owners must make their dogs' transition into their golden years as pleasant and rewarding as possible.

WHAT TO DO WHEN THE TIME COMES

You are never fully prepared to make a rational decision about putting your dog to sleep. It is very obvious that you love your Nova Scotia Duck Tolling Retriever or you would not be reading this book. Putting a beloved dog to sleep is extremely difficult. It is a decision that must be made with your vet. You are usually forced to make the decision when your dog experiences one or more life-threatening symptoms that have become serious enough for you to seek veterinary assistance.

If the prognosis of the malady indicates that the end is near and that your beloved pet will only continue to suffer and experience no enjoyment for the balance of its life, then euthanasia is the right choice.

WHAT IS EUTHANASIA?

Euthanasia derives from the Greek, meaning *good death*. In other words, it is the planned, painless killing of a dog suffering from a painful, incurable condition, or who is so aged that he cannot walk, see, eat or control his excretory functions. Euthanasia is usually accom-

plished by injection with an overdose of anesthesia or a barbiturate. Aside from the prick of the needle, the experience is usually painless.

MAKING THE DECISION

The decision to euthanize your dog is never easy. The days during which the dog becomes ill and the end occurs can be unusually stressful for you. If this is your first experience with the death of a loved one, you may need the comfort dictated by your religious beliefs. If you are the head of the family and have children, you should have involved them in the decision of putting your Toller to sleep. Usually your dog can be maintained on drugs for a few days in order to give you ample time to make a decision. During this time, talking with members of your family or with people who have lived through the same experience can ease the burden of your inevitable decision.

THE FINAL RESTING PLACE

Dogs can have some of the same privileges as humans. The

TALK IT OUT

The more openly your family discusses the whole stressful occurrence of the aging and eventual loss of a beloved pet, the easier it will be for you when the time comes.

remains of your beloved dog can be buried in a pet cemetery, which is generally expensive. If your dog has died at home, he can be buried in your yard in a suitable spot marked by a stone, flowers or a newly planted tree. Alternatively, your dog can be cremated individually and the ashes returned to you. A less expensive option is mass cremation, although, of course, the ashes cannot then be returned. Vets can usually help you locate a pet cemetery or arrange the cremation on your behalf. The cost of these options should always be discussed frankly and openly with your vet.

GETTING ANOTHER DOG?
The grief of losing your beloved dog will be as lasting as the grief of losing a human friend or relative. In most cases, if your dog died of old age (if there is such a thing), it had slowed down considerably. Do you want a new Toller puppy to replace it? Or are you better off finding a more mature Toller, say two to three years of age, which will usually

be house-trained and will have an already developed personality. In this case, you can find out if you like each other after a few hours of being together.

The decision is, of course, your own. Do you want another Toller or perhaps a different breed so as to avoid comparison with your beloved friend? Most people usually buy the same breed because they know (and love) the characteristics of that breed. Then, too, they often know people who have the same breed and perhaps they are lucky enough that a breeder they know and respect expects a litter soon. What could be better?

Many towns have pet cemeteries located nearby. Your vet can help you locate one if you choose this option.

Some pet cemeteries have facilities to store urns that contain dog's ashes after cremation.

SHOWING YOUR

NOVA SCOTIA DUCK TOLLING RETRIEVER

When you purchase your Toller, you will make it clear to the breeder whether you want one just as a lovable companion and pet, or if you hope to be buying a Toller with show prospects. No reputable breeder will sell you a young puppy and tell you that it is *definitely* of show quality, for so much can go wrong during the early months of a puppy's development. If you plan to show, what you will hopefully have acquired is a puppy with "show potential."

To the novice, exhibiting a Toller in the show ring may look easy, but it takes a lot of hard work and devotion to do top winning at conformation shows, not to mention a little luck too!

The first concept that the canine novice learns when watching a dog show is that each dog first competes against members of his own breed. Once the judge has selected the best member of each breed (Best of Breed), provided that the show is judged on a Group system, that chosen dog will compete with other Best of Breed dogs in his group. Finally, the dogs chosen first in each group will compete for Best in Show.

The second concept that you must understand is that the dogs are not actually compared against one another. The judge compares each dog against his breed standard. While some early breed standards were indeed based on specific dogs that were famous or popular, many dedicated enthusiasts say that a perfect specimen, as described in the standard, has never walked into a show ring, has never been bred and, to the woe of dog breeders around the globe, does not exist. Breeders attempt to get as close to this ideal as possible with every litter, but theoretically the "perfect" dog is so elusive that it is impossible (and if the "perfect" dog were born, breeders and judges would never agree that it was indeed "perfect!").

If you are interested in exploring the world of dog showing, your best bet is to join your local breed club or your country's national parent club, i.e., the Nova Scotia Duck Tolling Retriever Club of the US,

DUAL-PURPOSE BREED

The NSDTR Club in the USA was founded in 1984. Determined to maintain the Toller as a dual-purpose breed, the club awards championships only to dogs that have passed either the Natural Instinct Test (NIT) or the Working Certificate (WC).

The NIT consists of back-to-back single land marks, back-to-back single water marks and a tolling test. The WC consists of a land double mark, back-to-back water singles and a tolling test. In both cases, the tolling test requires the dog to retrieve an object on a shoreline at least six times in succession, and each retrieve must be done with the necessary animation to attract ducks, even though no ducks actually are used during the tolling test.

To locate the breed club closest to you, contact the national kennel club (in the US, the American Kennel Club; in Canada, the Canadian Kennel Club; in Britain, The Kennel Club), which furnishes the rules and regulations for all of these events plus general dog registration and other basic requirements of dog ownership.

If your Toller is of age and registered, you can enter him in a dog show where the breed is offered classes. Only unaltered dogs can be entered in a dog show, so if you have spayed or neutered your Toller, you cannot compete in conformation shows. The reason for this is simple. Dog shows are the main forum to prove which representatives in a breed are worthy of being bred.

The Toller's natural beauty shines through in the show ring, although just as important is that the breed retains its natural working abilities.

Canada, Great Britain, etc. These clubs often host both regional and national specialties, shows only for Tollers, which can include conformation as well as agility or working trials. Even if you have no intention of competing with your Toller, a specialty is like a festival for lovers of the breed who congregate to share their favorite topic: Nova Scotia Duck Tolling Retrievers! Clubs also send out newsletters, and some organize training days and seminars in order that people may learn more about their chosen breed.

Showing your Toller requires preparation on the part of both dog and handler. This Toller stays focused on his handler as he "stacks" or stands, looking his best for the judge.

Only dogs that have achieved championships—the recognized "seal of approval" for quality in pure-bred dogs—should be bred. Altered dogs, however, can participate in other events such as obedience trials and the Canine Good Citizen program.

Before you actually step into the ring, you would be well advised to sit back and observe the judge's ring procedure. If it is your first time in the ring, do not be over-anxious and run to the front of the line. It is much better to stand back and study how the exhibitor in front of you is performing.

The judge asks each handler to "stack" the dog, hopefully showing the dog off to his best advantage. The judge will observe the dog from a distance and from different angles, and approach the dog to check his teeth, overall structure, alertness and muscle tone, as well as consider how well the dog "conforms" to the standard. Most importantly, the judge will have the exhibitor move the dog around the ring in some pattern that he should specify (another advantage to not going first, but always listen since some judges change their directions—and the judge is always right!). Finally, the judge will give the dog one last look before moving on to the next exhibitor.

If you are not in the top four in your class at your first show, do not be discouraged. Be patient and consistent, and you may eventually find yourself in a winning line-up. Remember that the winners were once in your shoes and have devoted many hours and much money to earn the placement. If you find that your dog is losing every time and never getting a nod, it may be time to consider a different dog sport or to just enjoy your Toller as a pet. Parent clubs offer other events, such as agility, tracking, obedience, instinct tests and more, which may be of interest to the owner of a well-trained Toller.

OBEDIENCE TRIALS
Obedience trials in the US trace back to the early 1930s when organized obedience training was developed to demonstrate how well dog and owner could work together. The pioneer of obedience trials is Mrs. Helen Whitehouse Walker, a Standard Poodle fancier, who designed a series of exercises after the Associated Sheep, Police Army Dog Society of Great Britain. Since the days of Mrs. Walker, obedience trials have grown by leaps and bounds, and today there are over 2,000 trials with more than 100,000 dogs competing each year, and that's in the US alone! Any registered dog can enter an obedience trial, regardless of conformational disqualifications or neutering.

Obedience trials are divided into three levels of progressive difficulty. At the first level, the Novice, dogs compete for the title Companion Dog (CD); at the intermediate level, the Open, dogs compete for the title Companion Dog Excellent (CDX); and at the advanced level, dogs compete for the title Utility Dog (UD). Classes are sub-divided into "A" (for beginners) and "B" (for more experienced handlers). A perfect score at any level is 200, and a dog must score 170 or better to earn a "leg," of which three are needed to earn the title. To earn points, the dog must score more than 50% of the available points in each exercise; the possible points range from 20 to 40.

Once a dog has earned the UD title, he can compete with other proven obedience dogs for the coveted title of Utility Dog Excellent (UDX), which requires that the dog win "legs" in ten shows. Utility Dogs who earn "legs" in Open B and Utility B earn points toward their

WORKING TITLES

The titles available to the working Toller include: Companion Dog (CD), no track required; Utility Dog (UD), 30-minute-old track; Working Dog (WD), 90-minute-old track; Tracking Dog (TD), 180-minute-old track; and Patrol Dog (PD), which involves manwork, not a recommended activity for the soft-natured Toller.

Obedience Trial Champion title. In 1977, the title Obedience Trial Champion (OTCh.) was established by the AKC. To become an OTCh., a dog needs to earn 100 points, which requires three first places in Open B and Utility under three different judges.

AGILITY TRIALS

Having had its origins in the UK back in 1977, AKC agility had its official beginning in the US in August 1994, when the first licensed agility trials were held. The AKC allows all registered breeds (including Miscellaneous Class breeds) to participate, providing the dog is 12 months of age or older. Agility is designed so that the handler demonstrates how well the dog can work at his side. The handler directs his dog over an obstacle course that includes jumps (such as those used in agility trials), as well as tires, the dog walk, weave poles, pipe tunnels, collapsed tunnels, etc. While working their way through the course, the dog must keep one eye and ear on the handler and the rest of his body on the course. The handler gives verbal and hand signals to guide the dog through the course.

The first organization to promote agility trials in the US was the United States Dog Agility Association, Inc. (USDAA), which was established in 1986 and spawned numerous member clubs around the country. Both the USDAA and the AKC offer titles to winning dogs.

Agility is great fun for dog and owner in countries world-wide, with many rewards for everyone involved. Interested owners should join a training club that has obstacles and experienced agility handlers who can introduce you and your dog to the "ropes" (and tires, tunnels, etc.).

WORKING TRIALS

The agile little Toller is an excellent candidate for working trials in Canada, the US, the UK and other countries that offer such venues to prove a dog's worth as a working dog and partner. Working trials provide an energetic outlet for any Toller who has had some measure of obedience training and who enjoys a higher level of physical activity.

In working trials, the dogs compete against a standard of performance rather than each other. The degree of difficulty increases with each working class. The tests combine exercises in obedience (heeling on- and off-lead and the send-away; static exercises of sit and down), agility tests of jumping, scaling and recalls, retrieving exercises and nosework that includes the search and tracking of articles. Dogs must earn at least 70% in their group in order to qualify and earn the corresponding certificate.

INFORMATION ON CLUBS

You can get information about dog shows from the national kennel clubs:

Canadian Kennel Club
89 Skyway Ave., Suite 100, Etobicoke, Ontario
M9W 6R4 Canada
www.ckc.ca

American Kennel Club
5580 Centerview Dr., Raleigh, NC 27606-3390
www.akc.org

The Kennel Club
1-5 Clarges St., Piccadilly, London W1Y 8AB
UK
www.the-kennel-club.org.uk

Fédération Cynologique Internationale
14, rue Leopold II, B-6530 Thuin, Belgium
www.fci.be

FÉDÉRATION CYNOLOGIQUE INTERNATIONALE

Established in 1911, the Fédération Cynologique Internationale (FCI) represents the "world kennel club." This international body brings uniformity to the breeding, judging and showing of pure-bred dogs. Although the FCI originally included only five European nations: France, Germany, Austria, the Netherlands and Belgium (which remains its headquarters), the organization today embraces nations on six continents and recognizes well over 300 breeds of pure-bred dog.

The FCI sponsors both national and international shows. The hosting country determines the judging system and breed standards are always based on the breed's country of origin. Dogs from every country can participate in these impressive canine spectacles, the largest of which is the World Dog Show, hosted in a different country each year.

There are three titles attainable through the FCI: the International Champion, which is the most prestigious; the International Beauty Champion, which is based on aptitude certificates in different countries; and the International Trial Champion, which is based on achievement in obedience trials in different countries. An FCI title requires a dog to win three CACs (*Certificats d'Aptitude au Championnat*) at regional or club shows under three different judges who are breed specialists. The title of International Champion is gained by winning four CACIBs (*Certificats d'Aptitude au Championnat International de Beauté*), which are offered only at international shows, with at least a one-year lapse between the first and fourth award.

The FCI is divided into ten groups. At the World Dog Show, the following classes are offered for each breed: Puppy Class (6–9 months), Junior Class (9–18 months), Open Class (15 months or older) and Champion Class. A dog can be awarded a classification of Excellent, Very Good, Good, Sufficient and Not Sufficient. Puppies can be awarded classifications of Very Promising, Promising or Not Promising. Four placements are made in each class. After all classes are judged, a Best of Breed is selected. Other special groups and classes may also be shown. Each exhibitor showing a dog receives a written evaluation from the judge.

Besides the World Dog Show and other all-breed shows, you can exhibit your dog at specialty shows held by different breed clubs. Specialty shows may have their own regulations. To find out more about the FCI or this year's World Dog Show, visit the club's website on the Internet at fci.be.

NOVA SCOTIA DUCK TOLLING RETRIEVER

As a Nova Scotia Duck Tolling Retriever owner, you have selected your dog so that you and your loved ones can have a companion, a friend and a four-legged family member. You invest time, money and effort to care for and train the family's new charge. Of course, this chosen canine behaves perfectly! Well, perfectly like a *dog*.

THINK LIKE A DOG
Dogs do not think like humans, nor do humans think like dogs, though we try. Unfortunately, a dog is incapable of comprehending how humans think, so the responsibility falls on the owner to adopt a proper canine mind-set. Dogs cannot rationalize and only exist in the present moment. Many a dog owner makes the mistake in training of thinking that he can reprimand his dog for something the dog did a while ago. Basically, you cannot even reprimand a dog for something he did 20 seconds ago! Either catch him in the act or forget it! It is a waste of your and your dog's time—in his mind, you are reprimanding him for whatever he is doing at that moment.

The following behavioral problems represent some which owners most commonly encounter. Every dog is unique and every situation is unique. No author could purport for you to solve your Toller's problems simply by reading a chapter in a book. Here we outline some basic "dogspeak" so that owners' chances of solving behavioral problems are increased.

Discuss bad habits with your vet and he/she can recommend a behavioral specialist to consult

> **SMILE!**
> Dogs and humans may be the only animals that smile. A dog will imitate the smile on his owner's face when he greets a friend. The dog only smiles at his human friends; he never smiles at another dog or cat. Usually, a dog rolls up his lips and shows his teeth in a clenched mouth while rolling over onto his back, begging for a soft scratch.

in appropriate cases. Since behavioral abnormalities are the main reason for owners' abandoning their pets, we hope that you will make a valiant effort to solve your Toller's problems if they occur. Patience and understanding are virtues that must dwell in every pet-loving household.

SEPARATION ANXIETY

Recognized by behaviorists as the most common form of stress for dogs, separation anxiety can also lead to destructive behaviors in your dog. It's more than your Toller's howling his displeasure at your leaving the house and his being left alone. This is a normal reaction, no different from the child who cries as his mother leaves him on the first day at school. Separation anxiety, however, is

"I'm so happy to see you!" Remember that puppies are babies and need the security of having someone nearby. As your Toller gets older, he should become able to spend time alone without nervousness or unease.

> **I'M HOME!**
> Dogs left alone for varying lengths of time may often react wildly when their owners return. Sometimes they run, jump, bite, chew, tear things apart, wet themselves, gobble their food or behave in very undisciplined ways. If your dog behaves in this manner upon your return home, allow him to calm down before greeting him or he will consider your attention as a reward for his antics.

more serious. In fact, if you are constantly with your dog, he will come to expect you with him all of the time, making it even more traumatic for him when you are not there.

Obviously, you enjoy spending time with your dog, and he thrives on your love and attention. However, it should not become a dependent relationship in which he is heartbroken without you. This broken heart can also bring on destructive behavior as well as loss of appetite, depression and lack of interest in play and interaction. Canine behaviorists have spent much time and energy to help owners better understand the significance of this stressful condition.

One thing you can do to minimize separation anxiety is to make your entrances and exits as low-key as possible. Do not give your dog a long drawn-out good-

bye, and do not lavish him with hugs and kisses when you return. This is giving in to the attention that he craves, and it will only make him miss it more when you are away. Another thing you can try is to give your dog a treat when you leave; this will not only keep him occupied and keep his mind off the fact that you have just left, but it will also help him associate your leaving with a pleasant experience.

You may have to accustom your dog to being left alone at intervals. Of course, when your dog starts whimpering as you approach the door, your first instinct will be to run to him and comfort him, but do not do it! Eventually he will adjust to your absence. His anxiety stems from being placed in an unfamiliar situation; by familiarizing him with being alone, he will learn that he will survive. That is not to say you should purposely leave your dog home alone, but the dog needs to know that, while he can depend on you for his care, you do not have to be by his side 24 hours a day. Some behaviorists recommend tiring the dog out before you leave home—take him for a good long walk or engage in a game of fetch in the yard.

When the dog is alone in the house, he should be placed in his crate—another distinct advantage to crate-training your dog. The crate should be placed in his familiar happy family area, where he normally sleeps and already feels comfortable, thereby making him feel more at ease when he is alone. Be sure to give the dog a special chew toy to enjoy while he settles into his crate.

AGGRESSION

This is a problem that concerns all responsible dog owners. Aggression can be a very big problem in dogs, and, when not controlled, always becomes

---

DOGS HAVE FEELINGS, TOO

You probably don't realize how much your dog notices the presence of a new person in your home as well as the loss of a familiar face. If someone new has moved in with you, your pet will need help adjusting. Have the person feed your dog or accompany the two of you on a walk. Also, make sure your roommate is aware of the rules and routines you have already set for your dog.

If you have just lost a longtime companion, there is a chance you could end up with a case of "leave me, leave my dog." Dogs experience separation anxiety and depression, so watch for any changes in sleeping and eating habits and try to lavish a little extra love on your dog. It might make you feel better too.

dangerous. An aggressive dog, no matter the size, may lunge at, bite or even attack a person or another dog. Fortunately, the Toller is a non-aggressive breed by nature; aloofness upon first meetings is normal and should not be mistaken for aggression. However, every dog owner should know how to recognize and correct aggressive behavior, should it occur.

Aggressive behavior is not to be tolerated. It is more than just inappropriate behavior; it is painful for a family to watch their dog become unpredictable in his behavior to the point where they are afraid of him. While not all aggressive behavior is dangerous, growling, baring teeth, etc., can be frightening. It is important to ascertain why the dog is acting in this manner. Aggression is a display of dominance, and the dog should not have the dominant role in his pack, which is, in this case, your family.

It is important not to challenge an aggressive dog, as this could provoke an attack. Observe your Toller's body language. Does he make direct eye contact and stare? Does he try to make himself as large as possible: ears pricked, chest out, tail erect? Height and size signify authority in a dog pack—being taller or "above" another dog literally means that he is "above" in

DOMINANT AGGRESSION

Never allow your puppy to growl at you or bare his tiny teeth. Such behavior is dominant and aggressive. If not corrected, the dog will repeat the behavior, which will become more threatening as he grows larger and will eventually lead to biting.

social status. These body signals tell you that your Toller thinks he is in charge, a problem that needs to be addressed. An aggressive dog is unpredictable; you never know when he is going to strike and what he is going to do. You cannot understand why a dog that is playful one minute is growling the next.

Fear is a common cause of aggression in dogs. Perhaps your Toller had a negative experience as a puppy, which causes him to be fearful when a similar situation presents itself later in life. The dog may act aggressively in order to protect himself from whatever is making him afraid. It is not always easy to determine what is making your dog fearful, but if you can isolate what brings out the fear reaction, you can help the dog get over it.

Supervise your Toller's interactions with people and other dogs, and praise the dog when it goes well. If he starts to act aggressively in a situation, correct him and remove him

Littermates are built-in teachers of the "rules of the pack." Puppy rough-housing is normal behavior; it's one way to see who comes out on top.

from the situation. Do not let people approach the dog and start petting him without your express permission. That way, you can have the dog sit to accept petting, and praise him when he behaves properly. You are focusing on praise and on modifying his behavior by rewarding him when he acts appropriately. By being gentle and by supervising his interactions, you are showing him that there is no need to be afraid or defensive.

If your Toller does display aggressive behavior and you are having trouble modifying it, the best solution is to consult a behavioral specialist, one who has experience with the retriever breeds, and the Toller specifically if possible. Together,

NO EYE CONTACT

If you and your on-lead dog are approached by a larger, running dog that is not restrained, walk away from the dog as quickly as possible. Do not allow your dog to make eye contact with the other dog. You should not make eye contact either. In dog terms, eye contact indicates a challenge.

The nose knows! Dogs of all ages use their acute sense of smell to figure things out, such as finding their toilet area, detecting the presence of other dogs, etc.

season lasting about three weeks. These are the only times in which a female dog will mate, and she usually will not allow this until the second week of the cycle, although this varies from bitch to bitch. If not bred during the heat cycle, it is not uncommon for a bitch to experience a false pregnancy, in which her mammary glands swell and she exhibits maternal tendencies toward toys or other objects.

With male dogs, owners must be aware that whole dogs (dogs who are not neutered)

perhaps you can pinpoint the cause of your dog's aggression and do something about it.

SEXUAL BEHAVIOR

Dogs exhibit certain sexual behaviors that may have influenced your choice of male or female when you first purchased your Nova Scotia Duck Tolling Retriever. To a certain extent, spaying/neutering will eliminate these behaviors, but if you are purchasing a dog that you wish to breed from, you should be aware of what you will have to deal with throughout the dog's life.

Female dogs usually have two estruses per year, with each

"X" MARKS THE SPOT

As a pack animal, your dog marks his territory as a way of letting any possible intruders know that this is his space and that he will defend his territory if necessary. Your dog marks by urinating because urine contains pheromones that allow other canines to identify him. While this behavior seems like a nuisance, it speaks volumes about your dog's mental health. Stable, well-trained dogs living in quiet, less populated areas may mark less frequently than less confident dogs inhabiting busy urban areas that attract many possible invaders. If your dog only marks in certain areas in your home, such as your bed or the front door, these are the areas he feels obligated to defend. If your dog marks frequently, see your vet or an animal behaviorist.

have the natural inclination to mark their territory. Males mark their territory by spraying small amounts of urine as they lift their legs in a macho ritual. Marking can occur both outdoors in the garden and around the neighborhood as well as indoors on furniture legs, curtains and the sofa. Such behavior can be very frustrating for the owner; early training is strongly urged before the "urge" strikes your dog. Neutering the male at an appropriate early age can solve this problem before it becomes a habit.

Other problems associated with males are wandering and mounting. Both of these habits, of course, belong to the unneutered dog, whose sexual drive leads him away from home in search of the bitch in heat. Males will mount females in heat, as well as any other dog, male or female, that happens to catch their fancy. Other possible mounting partners include his owner, the furniture, guests to the home and strangers on the street. Discourage such behavior early on.

Owners must further recognize that mounting is not merely a sexual expression but also one of dominance, seen in both males and females alike. Be consistent and be persistent, and you will find that you can "move mounters."

NO BUTTS ABOUT IT!
Dogs get to know each other by sniffing each other's backsides. It seems that each dog has a telltale odor, probably created by the anal glands. It also distinguishes sex and signals when a female will be receptive to a male's attention. Some dogs snap at another dog's intrusion of their private parts.

CHEWING
The national canine pastime is chewing! Every dog loves to sink his "canines" into a tasty bone, so it is important to provide your dog with appropriate chew toys so that he doesn't destroy your possessions or make a habit of gnawing on your hands and toes. Although Tollers are not known for being voracious chewers, all dogs need to chew to massage their gums, to make their new teeth feel better and to exercise their jaws. This is a natural behavior that is deeply embedded in all things canine.

Our role as owners is not to stop our dogs' chewing, but rather to redirect it to positive, chew-worthy objects. Be an informed owner and purchase reliable chew toys, like strong nylon bones, that will not splinter. Be sure that the objects are safe and durable, since your dog's safety is at risk. Again, the owner is responsible for ensuring

NO JUMPING

Stop a dog from jumping up before he jumps. If he is getting ready to jump onto you, simply walk away. If he jumps up on you before you can turn away, lift your knee so that it bumps him in the chest. Do not be forceful. Your dog soon will realize that jumping up is not a productive way of getting attention.

a dog-proof environment.

The best answer is prevention; that is, put your shoes, handbags and other tasty objects in their proper places (out of the reach of the growing canine mouth). Direct puppies to their toys whenever you see them "tasting" the furniture legs or the leg of your pants. Make a loud noise to attract the pup's attention and immediately escort him to his chew toy and engage him with the toy for at least four minutes, praising and encouraging him all the while. An array of safe, interesting chew toys will keep your dog's mind and teeth occupied, and distracted from chewing on things he shouldn't.

Some trainers recommend deterrents, such as hot pepper, a bitter spice or a product designed for this purpose, to discourage the dog from chewing unwanted objects. Test these products to see which works best before investing in large quantities.

JUMPING UP

Jumping up is a dog's friendly way of saying hello! Some dog owners do not mind when their dog jumps up. The problem arises when guests come to the house and the dog greets them in the same manner—whether they like it or not! However friendly the greeting may be, the chances are that your visitors will not appreciate your dog's enthusiasm. The dog will not be able to distinguish upon whom he can jump and whom he cannot. Therefore, it is probably best to discourage this behavior entirely.

Pick a command such as "Off" (avoid using "Down" since you will use that for the dog to lie down) and tell him "Off" when he jumps up. Place him on the ground on all fours and have him sit, praising him the whole time. Always lavish him with praise and petting when he is in the sit position. In this way, you can give him a warm affectionate greeting, let him know that you are as excited to see him as he is to see you and instill good manners at the same time!

DIGGING

Digging, which is seen as a destructive behavior to humans, is actually quite a natural behavior in dogs. Although terriers (the "earth dogs") are most associated with the digging, any

Save yourself and your belongings from the ravages of puppy teeth by providing your young Toller with an array of safe toys and encouraging him to use them.

dog's desire to dig can be irrepressible and most frustrating to his owners. When digging occurs in your garden, it is actually a normal behavior redirected into something the dog can do in his everyday life. In the wild, a dog would be actively seeking food, making his own shelter, etc. He would be using his paws in a purposeful manner for his survival. Since you provide him with food and shelter, he has no need to use his paws for these purposes, and so the energy that he would be using may manifest itself in the form of little holes all over your yard and flower beds.

Perhaps your dog is digging as a reaction to boredom—it is somewhat similar to someone eating a whole bag of chips in front of the TV—because they are there and there is nothing better to do! Boredom and lack of attention from their owners are the main reasons for Tollers to dig. Basically, the answer is to

SET AN EXAMPLE

Never scream, shout, jump or run about if you want your dog to stay calm. You set the example for your dog's behavior in most circumstances. Learn from your dog's reaction to your behavior and act accordingly.

provide the dog with adequate attention, play and exercise so that his mind and paws are occupied, and so that he feels as if he is doing something useful.

Of course, digging is easiest to control if it is stopped as soon as possible, but it is often hard to catch a dog in the act. If your dog is a compulsive digger and is not easily distracted by other activities, you can designate an area on your property where he is allowed to dig. If you catch him digging in an off-limits area of the yard, immediately take him to the approved area and praise him for digging there. Keep a close eye on him so that you can catch him in the act—that is the only way to make him understand what is permitted and what is not. If you take him to a hole he dug an hour ago and tell him "No," he will understand that you are not fond of holes, dirt or flowers. If you catch him while he is stifle-deep in your tulips, that is when he will get your message.

BARKING

Dogs cannot talk—oh, what they would say if they could! Instead, barking is a dog's way of "talking." It can be somewhat frustrating because it is not always easy to tell what a dog means by his bark—is he excited, happy, frightened or angry? Whatever it is that the dog is trying to say, he should not be punished for barking. It is only when the barking becomes excessive, and when the excessive barking becomes a bad habit, that the behavior needs to be modified.

Fortunately, Tollers are not particularly vocal dogs; they tend to use their barks more purposefully. If an intruder came into your home in the middle of the night and your Toller barked a warning, wouldn't you be pleased? You would probably deem your dog a hero, a wonderful watchdog. On the other hand, if a friend drops by unexpectedly, rings the doorbell and is greeted with a sudden sharp bark, you would probably be annoyed at the dog. But in reality, isn't this just the same behavior? The dog does not know any better. Unless he sees

DOG TALK

Deciphering your dog's barks is very similar to understanding a baby's cries: there is a different cry for eating, sleeping, potty needs, etc. Your dog talks to you not only through howls and groans but also through his body language. Baring teeth, staring and inflating the chest are all threatening gestures. If a dog greets you by licking his nose, turning his head or yawning, these are friendly, peacemaking gestures.

Fortunately for Toller owners, the breed is even-tempered and intelligent, looking to their masters for instruction and guidance.

HE'S PROTECTING YOU

Barking is your dog's way of protecting you. If he barks at a stranger walking past your house, a moving car or a fleeing cat, he is merely exercising his responsibility to protect his pack (*you*) and territory from a perceived intruder. Since the "intruder" usually keeps going, the dog thinks his barking chased it away and he feels fulfilled. This behavior leads your overly vocal friend to believe that he is the "dog in charge."

who is at the door and it is someone he knows, he will bark as a means of vocalizing that his (and your) territory is being threatened. While your friend is not posing a threat, it is all the same to the dog. Barking is his means of letting you know that there is an intrusion, whether friend or foe, on your property. This type of barking is instinctive and should not be discouraged.

Excessive habitual barking, though not generally a problem in the Toller, is a problem that should be corrected early on. As your Toller grows up, you will be able to tell when his barking is

purposeful and when it is for no reason. You will become able to distinguish your dog's different barks and their meanings. For example, the bark when someone comes to the door will be different than the bark when he is excited to see you. It is similar to a person's tone of voice, except that the dog has to rely totally on tone of voice because he does not have the benefit of using words. An incessant barker will be evident at an early age.

There are some things that encourage a dog to bark. For example, if your dog barks nonstop for a few minutes and you give him a treat to quiet him, he believes that you are rewarding him for barking. He will associate barking with getting a treat and will keep doing it until he is rewarded. On the other hand, if you give him a command such as "Quiet" and praise him after he has stopped barking for a few seconds, he will get the idea that being "quiet" is what you want him to do.

FOOD STEALING
Is your dog devising ways of stealing food from your coffee table or kitchen counter? If so, you must answer the following questions: Is your Toller a bit hungry, or is he "constantly famished" like many dogs seem to be? Face it, some dogs are more food-motivated than others.

The easiest way to prevent food stealing is not to give the dog access to any food to steal!

They are totally obsessed by the smell of food and can only think of their next meal. Food stealing is terrific fun and always yields a great reward—FOOD, glorious food.

Your goal as an owner, therefore, is to be sensible about where food is placed in the home and to reprimand your dog whenever he is caught in the act of stealing. But remember, only reprimand your dog if you actually see him stealing, not later when the crime is discovered; that will be of no use at all and will only serve to confuse him.

BEGGING

Just like food stealing, begging is a favorite pastime of hungry puppies! It achieves that same terrific result—FOOD! Dogs quickly learn that their owners keep the "good food" for themselves, and that we humans do not dine on dry food alone. Begging is a conditioned response related to a specific stimulus, time and place. The sounds of the kitchen, cans and

AIN'T MISBEHAVIN'

Punishment is rarely necessary for a misbehaving dog. Dogs that habitually behave badly probably had a poor education and do not know what is expected of them. They need training. Negative reinforcement on your part usually does more harm than good.

bottles opening, crinkling bags, the smell of food in preparation, etc., will excite the dog, and soon the paws will be in the air!

Here is the solution to stopping this behavior: Never give in to a beggar! You are rewarding the dog for sitting pretty, jumping up, whining and rubbing his nose into you by giving him food. By ignoring the dog, you will (eventually) force the behavior into extinction. Note that the behavior is likely to get worse before it disappears, so be sure there are not any "softies" in the family who will give in to little "Oliver" every time he whimpers, "More, please."

COPROPHAGIA

Feces eating is, to humans, one of the most disgusting behaviors that their dogs could engage in; yet, to dogs, it is perfectly normal. It is hard for us to understand why a dog would want to eat his own feces. He could be seeking certain nutrients that are missing from his diet, he could be just hungry or he could be attracted by the pleasing (to a dog) scent. While coprophagia most often refers to the dog's eating his own feces, a dog may just as likely eat that of another animal as well if he comes across it. Dogs often find the stool of cats and horses more palatable than that of other dogs.

Vets have found that diets with low levels of digestibility, containing relatively low levels of fiber and high levels of starch, increase coprophagia. Therefore, high-fiber diets may decrease the likelihood of dogs' eating feces. Both the consistency of the stool (how firm it feels in the dog's mouth) and the presence of undigested nutrients increase the likelihood. Once the dog develops diarrhea from feces eating, he will likely stop this distasteful habit.

To discourage this behavior, first make sure that the food you are feeding your dog is nutrition-

BE NOT AFRAID

Just like humans, dogs can suffer from phobias including fear of thunder, fear of heights, fear of stairs or even fear of specific objects such as the swimming pool. To help your dog get over his fear, first determine what is causing the phobia. For example, your dog may be generalizing by associating an accident that occurred on one set of stairs with every step he sees. You can try desensitization training, which involves introducing the fear-trigger to your dog slowly, in a relaxed setting, and rewarding him when he remains calm. Most importantly, when your dog responds fearfully, do not coddle or try to soothe him, as this only makes him think that his fear is okay.

PHARMACEUTICAL FIX

There are two drugs specifically designed to treat mental problems in dogs. About seven million dogs each year are destroyed because owners can no longer tolerate their dogs' behavior, according to Nicholas Dodman, a specialist in animal behavior at Tufts University in Massachusetts.

The first drug, Clomicalm, is prescribed for dogs suffering from separation anxiety, which is said to cause them to react when left alone by barking, chewing their owners' belongings, drooling copiously or defecating or urinating inside the home.

The second drug, Anipryl, is recommended for cognitive dysfunction syndrome or "old dog syndrome," a mental deterioration that comes with age. Such dogs often seem to forget that they were house-trained and where their food bowls are, and they may even fail to recognize their owners.

A tremendous human-animal bonding relationship is established with all dogs, particularly senior dogs. This precious relationship deteriorates when the dog does not recognize his master. The drug can restore the bond and make senior dogs feel more like their "old selves."

A happy, healthy Toller is well cared for and always ready for fun. Behavior problems are uncommon with active, interactive Tollers.

ally complete and that he is getting enough food. If changes in his diet do not seem to work, and no medical cause can be found, you will have to modify the behavior through environmental control before it becomes a habit. The best way to prevent your dog from eating his stool is to make it unavailable—clean up after he eliminates and remove any stool from the yard. If it is not there, he cannot eat it.

Reprimanding for stool eating rarely impresses the dog. Vets recommend distracting the dog while he is in the act of stool eating. Coprophagia is seen most frequently in pups 6 to 12 months of age, and usually disappears around the dog's first birthday.

INDEX

INDEX

My Nova Scotia
Duck Tolling Retriever

PUT YOUR PUPPY'S FIRST PICTURE HERE

Birth Date _____

Breeder's Name _____

Breeder's Address _____

Breeders Phone _____

Registration/ID Number _____

Distinguishing Features _____

Vet's Name _____

Vet's Address _____

Vet's Phone _____

VACCINATION RECORD				
Vaccine	Dates			